Stolen Kingdom

An American Conspiracy

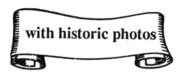

with historic photos

by Rich Budnick

Introduction by
Hawai'i Governor John Waihee

Stolen Kingdom
An American Conspiracy

Published by

Aloha Press
P.O. Box 4183
Honolulu, HI 96812

Library of Congress Catalog Card Number 92-072203
   Budnick, Rich
   ISBN NO. 0-944081-02-9

Book Cover Design by Debra Castro and Richard Mishina

Photo on page 38 from U.S. Military Academy Museum
all other photos are from the Hawai'i State Archives

Table of Contents

4

Introduction

The history of the overthrow of the Hawaiian monarchy and of American annexation remains controversial a century later, although the documentary record is clear.

Contemporary native Hawaiian demands for sovereignty, reparations and related issues require us to learn about that past history.

This book addresses those momentous events of a century ago, providing a general discussion of Hawaii's fragile sovereignty in an imperial era, and focusing on the critical developments of the 1893 overthrow and 1898 annexation.

Particularly well-described is the critical role of United States diplomats in the American acquisition of Hawai'i and the unsuccessful efforts of President Grover Cleveland to restore the monarchy.

I commend this book to all who have an interest in the history of Hawai'i. This is a highly informative and timely book about the demise of the Hawaiian Kingdom.

John Waihee

Governor
State of Hawai'i

Acknowledgments

I want to express my grateful appreciation to Linda Delaney, of the Office of Hawaiian Affairs. She generously shared with me her knowledge of Hawai'i history and the imperialistic era.

I also want to express my thanks to Dr. Kekuni Blaisdell for reviewing the manuscript and offering many important suggestions.

Several people deserve appreciation for their assistance and advice: Bill Souza, Jeannie Thompson, Julie Schoen, Melody McKenzie, Maile Meyer, H. Rodger Betts, Byron Baker, Jim Manke, Governor John Waihee, and B.J. Wade.

A special thanks goes to Bob Holmes, for his encouragement and advice.

In addition, I appreciate the creative efforts of Debra Castro and Rich Mishina for designing an attractive book cover.

I also want to thank the staff of the University of Hawai'i Hamilton Library Pacific Room and the State Library Hawaiian Room.

I wish to acknowledge these helpful people of the Hawai'i State Archives: Jean Charbinnet, Allen Hoof, Della Kua'ana, Patricia Lai, Jolene Nakamatsu, Victoria Nihi, Gloria Riingen, Susan Shaner, Richard Thompson, Geoffrey White, and Darryl Yap.

Finally, I thank my wife, Min-Tzu for patiently allowing me the time to finish this book.

Foreword

This book began as a simple editing of the two-volume *Final Report of the Native Hawaiians Study Commission,* published in 1983 with limited distribution. The Commission was a presidentially appointed, nine-member panel which reported on the culture, needs, and concerns of native Hawaiians.

The full Commission agreed on the woeful social, educational and economic conditions of the Hawaiian people, but its members were divided over American complicity and wrong-doing concerning the 1893 monarchy overthrow, and its consequences.

Six Commissioners, all Cabinet Undersecretaries, submitted Volume I of the Final Report to Congress. The chapters on the monarchy overthrow were written by William Dudley and Donna Nelson of the U.S. Navy Historical Center.

The three native Hawaiian Commissioners – chairperson Kīna'u Boyd Kamali'i, Winona K. Beamer, and H. Rodger Betts – submitted a dissenting Volume II. The chapters on the overthrow were written by Linda K. Delaney and Melody K. MacKenzie.

Volume II relies more rigorously on primary sources: official correspondence, memoirs and Congressional testimony of key participants during the period of the overthrow and annexation.

This book, **Stolen Kingdom: An American Conspiracy**, expands upon the *Native Hawaiians Study Commission Report,* and presents several hundred candid and confidential quotes from the 1,400-page U.S. House Report, published in 1895. That House Report reprints the Blount Report, a valuable historic document of statements and messages from Hawaiian monarchs, U.S. presidents, cabinet and diplomatic officials, and a firsthand investigation of the overthrow.

A Fragile Kingdom
Seeks Respect

"Such has always been the case with large countries,
the small ones have been gobbled up."
—David Malo

Foreign Influence in Hawai'i

"Land ho!" shouted the voyage-weary but surprised young
sailor, standing high atop the mast of the British ship, *HMS
Resolution,* one calm January morning in 1778.

Captain James Cook had unexpectedly sighted Hawai'i, a
populated, two thousand year old, archipelago civilization,
where he would lose his life one year later.

After centuries of isolation, Hawai'i was thrust into the
1800's, a century distinguished by imperialism and industrialization. Foreign governments would threaten Hawaii's sovereignty through political and economic manipulation, and by
military force.

Hawaii's kings had a great deal to worry about. There were
bullying threats from the commanders of foreign warships, the
increasing commerce of whaling and trading ships – with their
rioting, drinking, womanizing sailors – and a growing foreign
population demanding more rights and privileges than the native
Hawaiians enjoyed.

How long would traditional Hawaiian civilization last?
Would the foreigners with their big guns destroy Hawai'i?

To protect and preserve the independence of this tiny Kingdom, Kings Kamehameha I and II looked to Great Britain for
protection.

A wise and visionary leader, Kamehameha I unified his island Kingdom by making friends with the foreigners who offered military advice and foreign guns. The cannons helped him to defeat his enemies. If Kamehameha I hadn't quickly grasped the benefits of trading with the foreigners, the people of Hawai'i might instead be honoring Chief Kahekili, whose flair for violence marked his conquest of all islands except Hawai'i and Kaua'i.

Kamehameha I asked England to establish a protectorate over Hawai'i Island in 1794, in exchange for a warship to help him fight his arch-rival, Chief Kahekili. British Captain George Vancouver encouraged this protectorate, but the British Government never ratified the cession agreement.[1]

Thirty years later, in 1824, Kamehameha II sailed to Great Britain to discuss a British protectorate with King George IV. The two kings never met. Kamehameha II died from a measles epidemic in London before negotiating a treaty.

King Kamehameha I

King Kamehameha II

Honolulu village (1816)

Kamehameha II was succeeded by his 11-year old brother Kamehameha III, who reigned 30 years, from 1825-1854. Kamehameha III ruled longer than any monarch in Hawaiian history.

For several years, a regency of two dominating women, first Ka'ahumanu, and then Kīna'u, ruled the Kingdom. American Christian missionaries influenced both women, but the young King Kamehameha III wavered between the religious traditions of his ancestors and Christianity.

Lost somewhere between two cultures, Kamehameha III spent a great deal of time worrying about foreign invasions. Unlike his grandfather who knew how to use foreigners to his advantage, Kamehameha III allowed powerful people to control his life, and the destiny of his Kingdom.

The influence of foreigners, especially the strong-willed American missionaries, led to: a system of written laws and a constitutional government, treaties with foreign governments, and a policy allowing private land ownership. Foreign influence also led to an attack on Hawaiian civilization, a modification of the Hawaiian language, and a legal "stealing" of the land.

By 1845, Honolulu had grown from a small village to a vital commercial center. Few of the 1,000 foreigners relinquished their foreign citizenship, although some became dual citizens of Hawai'i and their country of origin.

Native Hawaiians became disillusioned with the increasing number of foreign advisors in their government. The King received a petition from prominent native Hawaiians urging the dismissal of naturalized foreigners appointed to Kingdom jobs. Kamehameha III did not respond to the petition. However the American Board of Commissioners for Foreign Missions withdrew their support of any missionaries who assumed jobs in the Hawaiian Government.

In 1852, a missionary-inspired constitution declared the King as the "Supreme Executive Magistrate"[2] with authority to proclaim and repeal constitutions, and to appoint a Privy Council of Ministers (Cabinet members).

Warship Diplomacy

Hawaii's King was responsible for protecting his people, and maintaining the independence of his Kingdom. This was difficult to do when foreign encroachment threatened to destroy Hawaii's sovereignty.

An international rivalry soon developed among the United States, Great Britain, and France – each trying to assert its influence in the Island Kingdom. Hawaii's mid-Pacific location with good harbors made the Kingdom a convenient port-of-call for whaling, commercial and naval vessels.

In 1826, Hawai'i formally negotiated with the United States its first international treaty promoting navigation and friendship, but America failed to ratify these articles of agreement.

Two separate incidents, in 1839 and 1843, convinced King Kamehameha III to seek international alliances to protect Hawai'i against foreign aggression. In both instances, the commanders of French and English warships seized temporary possession of Hawai'i by threatening to fire their cannons if the King refused to relinquish his sovereignty.

Many times, Hawaii's foreign residents asked warship commanders to support their claims against Kingdom laws and practices. Tiny Hawai'i, helpless and harassed, was no match for foreign navies with their powerful cannons and military might.

Without protection, the Kingdom could not survive. The Lahainaluna-educated native Hawaiian scholar David Malo predicted such a problem. Malo wrote these prophetic words to Kīna'u, the kuhina nui (premier and co-ruler):

David Malo

You must not think that this is anything like olden

times, that you are the only chiefs and can leave things as they are...This is the reason. If a big wave comes in, large fishes will come from the dark ocean which you never saw before and when they see the small fishes they will eat them up; such also is the case with large animals, they will prey on the smaller ones. The ships of the white men have come, and smart people have arrived from the great countries which you have never seen before, they know our people are few in number and living in a small country; they will eat us up, such has always been the case with large countries, the small ones have been gobbled up.[3]

France: Laplace Threatens War

Relations with the French were particularly troublesome, largely a result of American Protestant missionary influences. These dogmatic Protestant missionaries persuaded Hawaiian rulers to prohibit the teaching of Catholicism, and to banish French Catholic missionaries who competed for native Hawaiian converts. France objected to this religious persecution and expulsion, and also to an 1838 law that heavily taxed imported wine.

The problem reached a crisis in July, 1839. Captain Cyrille Laplace, commander of a French warship, threatened war if Kamehameha III did not agree to his demands.

To avoid bloodshed, the King announced a policy of religious toleration, signed an agreement (known as the "Laplace Convention"), and paid a $20,000 penalty to assure religious freedom. The agreement also limited the Hawaiian King's powers: Frenchmen accused of "any crime whatever" would be judged by a jury of foreigners suggested by the French consul, and French merchandise was not to be prohibited nor taxed more than 5% of value.[4]

How could Hawai'i protect itself? The King and his Privy Council desperately wanted to stop foreign intimidation, so they negotiated formal treaties with powerful foreign governments that hopefully, would respect the treaties, and protect Hawai'i in time of crisis. In 1842, King Kamehameha III sent a three man delegation to secure formal recognition with the United States, Great Britain, and France.

U.S.: Tyler Doctrine

The Hawaiian delegation succeeded in the United States. In a letter of December 19, 1842 to the visiting Hawaiian delegation, U.S. Secretary of State Daniel Webster stated:

> The United States...are more interested in the fate of the islands, and of their Government, than any other nation can be...The Government of the Sandwich Islands ought to be respected; that no power ought either to take possession of the islands as a conquest, or...colonization, and that no power ought to seek for any undue control over the existing Government, or any exclusive privileges or preferences in matters of commerce.[5]

Just 11 days later, on December 30, the United States issued the "Tyler Doctrine," named for U.S. President John Tyler. The Tyler Doctrine was the first formal recognition of Hawaii's sovereignty and independence, although it was not a treaty, but a unilateral American policy. Just as the Monroe Doctrine warned Europe in 1823 not to meddle in the affairs of the Western Hemisphere, the Tyler Doctrine warned Europe not to annex Hawai'i.

President Tyler announced:

> ...the United States...seeks...no exclusive control over the Hawaiian Government, but is content with its independent existence...but should events hereafter arise to require it (the United States) to make a decided remonstrance against the adoption of an opposite policy, it will be done....[6]

More Troubles with England, France and California Revolutionaries

Armed with the Tyler Doctrine, the King's representatives traveled next to Europe, seeking diplomatic recognition. Unfortunately, their mission was interrupted by another serious incident known as the "Paulet Affair."

Lord George Paulet, captain of a British warship; under orders from the acting British consul, demanded the Hawaiian Government recognize British land claims and other interests in Hawai'i, including the composition of jury trials. Paulet threatened to fire his ship's 26 cannons on Honolulu if the grievances were not settled.

A frightened King Kamehameha III complained that Paulet's demands "embarrass our feeble government."[7] Kamehameha III considered ceding Hawai'i to France or the United States. Instead, he temporarily ceded the Islands "under protest"[8] to Great Britain on February 25, 1843. The King's cession was "subject to the decision" of the British Government "on the receipt of full information."[9]

Dr. Gerrit Judd, a physician and former American missionary now serving the King as Foreign Affairs Minister, wrote: "the King declared himself a dead man, and expressed his conviction that his ruin was determined."[10]

During this bewildering period of Paulet's protectorate, the British flag flew over Hawai'i. Dr. Judd secretly took important government papers to the Royal Mausoleum, where he used Ka'ahumanu's coffin as a desk to write appeals to England and the United States.

Six months later, on July 31, British Rear Admiral Richard Thomas recognized Kamehameha III as Hawaii's sovereign.

Four months later, England and France signed a joint declaration recognizing Hawaii's independence, and pledged to honor Hawaii's integrity if the other nation would. The declaration was signed in London, on November 11, 1843.

The United States refused to sign the treaty. America preferred to stand behind its Tyler Doctrine rather than break precedent and plunge into "entangling alliances" as U.S. President George Washington had warned against in 1796.

Hawai'i leaders learned that treaties could be negotiated, and treaties could be broken. The people of Hawai'i suffered as stronger nations routinely ignored treaties or coerced Hawai'i to sign inequitable treaties.

Powerful Britain and France continued to intimidate Hawai'i by imposing new treaties with objectionable trade preferences, and requiring that juries be limited to people from their own country.

In 1849, another power-hungry Admiral, Legorant de Tromelin of France ignored his nation's 1843 treaty, and demanded satisfaction for French complaints, mostly about liquor. De Tromelin's troops ransacked and seized government offices and the fort, and stole the King's yacht. As in the past, the weaker native government did not resist.

Unable to cope with these acts of French aggression,

Captain James Cook

Lord George Paulet

Kamehameha III sought additional protection from the United States, resulting in an 1849 Hawai'i-U.S. treaty of friendship, commerce, and navigation. The treaty, which America would break nearly a half-century later, promised "perpetual peace and amity between the United States and the King of the Hawaiian Islands, his heirs and successors."[11]

As America stepped forward to support Hawai'i, France's Minister to Hawai'i, Guillaume Dillon acknowledged: "The Sandwich Islands seem inevitably destined to come under the direct influence, if not a complete annexation, on the part of the United States."[12]

Two years later, in 1851, King Kamehameha III secretly pursued a treaty that would annex Hawai'i to the United States as a state.

Secret Annexation Treaty with U.S.

The deTromelin crisis deeply worried Kamehameha III that France would seize Hawai'i, just as it had taken Tahiti.

At the same time, Kamehameha III suffered from persistent rumors that lawless California adventurers who had been stirring-up revolutions in Latin America, would be coming to Hawai'i.

Historian W.D. Alexander wrote that a large California immigration "embraced many restless, ambitious spirits, some of whom came for the purpose of exciting revolution." He summarized the King's woes:

> (The King) had long been harassed by the threats of foreign powers; he had once been dethroned by a British naval force; he had repeatedly been compelled to make humiliating concessions at the cannon's mouth; and his difficulties with France still remained unsettled. At the same time he was kept in a state of alarm by rumors of (revolutionaries) from abroad and threats of conspirators at home to overturn his government.[13]

Robert Wyllie, a Scottish immigrant with aristocratic tendencies, replaced Dr. Judd as Minister of Foreign Affairs, a year after arriving in Hawai'i. Wyllie would hold that position for 20 years. He suggested to Judd:

> ...The tide of events rushes on to annexation to the United States – and for this very reason, that we Hawaiians are becoming fewer...every day, and the Americans in California more numerous and enterprising. When we die off they will occupy our places...As things are, if they should come here (from California), I fear they would feel it to be their interest to upset the Government, just as the Americans did in Texas.[14]

A melancholy King Kamehameha III – torn between the traditions of his ancestors, and the new ways of the missionaries – suffered as a lost soul trying to cope with two conflicting cultures. Troubles from annexationists, foreign aggression, the lack of an heir, and the rapid population decline of his people compounded his depression.

In desperation, Kamehameha III said the French aggression was "oppressive to my Kingdom" and sought security for his Kingdom through American statehood.[15] He sent a secret March 10, 1851 annexation proclamation to U.S. Commissioner Luther Severance asking for American protection, and in case of emergency, to cede Hawai'i to the United States.

This conditional deed of cession would not take effect if France settled its problems and treated the Hawaiian King as a sovereign. Otherwise, the cession would be "perpetual."[16]

By late March, the King proposed a secret treaty for annexation as an American state "to be instantly acted upon on the emergency of any sudden danger" of aggression from France. In a letter of appeal to the U.S. President from U.S. Commissioner Luther Severance and Hawai'i Foreign Affairs Minister Robert Wyllie, the King admitted "helplessness" and expressed fear of "lawless invasions" from France.

Kamehameha III said he would prefer to resign as Hawaiian sovereign than "continue to be the victim of aggression...the mere shadow of a King without power...." The King added, "I distrust France and fear her."[17]

Then in June, the Hawai'i Legislature adopted a resolution authorizing the King to place the Kingdom under protection of some friendly power if necessary, "to shield (the King) and his Kingdom from insult and oppression."[18]

Severance supported annexation, but his boss, U.S. Secretary of State Daniel Webster, opposed it. In a July 14 letter, the respected American statesman Webster, who had drafted the Tyler Doctrine, wrote:

> ...many American citizens have gone to settle in the islands; if so, they have ceased to be American citizens. The Government of the United States feel(s) an interest in them not extended to foreigners, but by the law of nations they have no right to further demand the protection of this Government.[19]

Webster added:

> You will therefore not encourage in them, nor indeed in any others, any idea or expectation that the island will become annexed to the United States...I do not suppose there is any immediate danger of any new menaces from France.[20]

Webster, the last American Secretary of State to treat Hawaii's sovereignty with a "hands-off" policy, told Severance to return the annexation document.

America's tough response to French policies was a "painful surprise" to French officials, wrote U.S. Minister to France Jean Rives to Webster, from Paris, on July 22, 1851. France suggested that rumors of French hostilities to Hawai'i were unfounded. Rives wrote: "France would always respect the independence of these islands..."[21] In other words, France had found out about Kamehameha's quiet annexation effort, and backed off.

The urgency for American annexation had quieted, but Kamehameha III made arrangements for a contingency plan in case a future emergency should develop.

He gave Dr. Gerrit Judd secret instructions to negotiate a protectorate and sale of Kingdom sovereignty to the United States.

A year later, Hawaii's new 1852 Constitution gave the King power to sell the Kingdom "if it was indispensable to free it from the insult and oppression of any foreign power."[22]

In Washington, the U.S. Senate learned of the secret effort to annex Hawai'i. The Senate twice asked President Millard Filmore to furnish documents about transferring Hawaiian sovereignty, but President Filmore ignored both requests.

For the first time, annexation was advocated in the U.S. Congress. Congressman J. McCorkle (D-California) declared on November 22, 1852 that Hawai'i was essential to protecting California's Pacific coast in time of war, and vital to trade with Asia and Pacific islands.[23]

A new U.S. President, Franklin Pierce moved into the White House in 1853. The expansion-minded Pierce wanted to annex both Cuba and Hawai'i.

In August, nearly two dozen European and American merchants and planters in Hawai'i petitioned Kamehameha III for annexation by honorable means. Some of the petitioners formed a secret committee which preferred a revolution.[24]

A month later, the British and French consuls in Hawai'i protested to the King that annexation would be unconstitutional, against international law, and "could not be looked upon with indifference by either the British or French Government."[25]

U.S. Secretary of State William Marcy spared no enthusiasm for annexation in this confidential November letter to William Miller, Britain's Foreign Minister:

...if the present Government of the Sandwich Islands must fall (to another government), and if their admission to this Union be desired, I will not conceal from you that it is highly probable that the Government as well as the Congress and the people of the United States would be disposed to receive them.[26]

In a letter of December 16, 1853, Marcy advised American diplomats in England and France: "I do not think the present Hawaiian Government can long remain in the hands of the present rulers or under the control of the native inhabitants of these islands...."

Marcy stressed that it would be "reasonable and fair" that those two nations should approve of American control of Hawai'i if sovereignty is transferred "by fair means".[27]

U.S. Secretary of State William Marcy wrote Commissioner to Hawai'i David Gregg an April 4, 1854 letter giving Gregg "full

King Kamehameha III   **King Kamehameha IV**

power" to draft a treaty "for the transfer of the Sandwich Islands to the United States." Marcy suggested paying Hawaii's royal family $100,000 to surrender their political sovereignty. Marcy wrote:

> It appears by your dispatches lately...that the ruling authorities of the Hawaiian Government have become convinced of their inability to sustain themselves any longer as an independent State, and are prepared to throw themselves upon our protection or to seek incorporation into our political system.[28]

Kamehameha III felt overwhelmed by fear that foreign harassment and "sudden danger" would threaten Hawaii's sovereignty. Through most of 1854, the Hawaiian Government and U.S. Commissioner David Gregg negotiated a secret annexation treaty with the United States.[29]

Under the treaty terms being pursued, the King and others in royal succession would share annual annuities of $300,000 from the United States, plus an annual stipend of $75,000 for 10 years to support schools and education.[30]

Robert Wyllie, Hawaii's Foreign Affairs Minister wrote to Hawai'i Supreme Court Chief Justice William Lee on July 11, 1854: "Under such a clear necessity, colonial subjection to any European power would not be so favorable to the interests of the islands as their admission as a sovereign state of the United States."[31]

In the end, annexation as a state would not be accomplished. Secretary of State Marcy informed U.S. Minister Gregg about "strong objections" to statehood."[32] U.S. President Pierce told Lee, "the United States did not desire to annex the Islands...(since) it would be entering upon a quasi-colonial system...of very doubtful policy."[33]

England and France would have opposed statehood, which would have been difficult to accomplish anyway, during an era when each new state was carefully admitted as either slave or free, and only after great political compromises were made. Southern states would have objected to admitting Hawai'i as a non-slave state, since Hawai'i is located below the Mason-Dixon line.

The secret treaty ultimately failed with the death of Kamehameha III on December 15, 1854. His nephew and successor, Prince Alexander Liholiho, who reigned as Kamehameha IV from 1854-1863, did not reopen discussions for an annexation treaty.

Kamehameha IV Seeks a Reciprocity Treaty

The new King and his wife Queen Emma, were decidedly pro-British, and turned away from American influence. Queen Emma had been adopted by a British physician, was married in a British ceremony, and helped to establish a branch of the Church of England in Hawai'i.

Kamehameha IV had other reasons to dislike America.

As an impressionable but proud young Prince traveling in the United States in 1850, the 15-year old Liholiho fell victim to the ugliness of racial prejudice near Washington, D.C. A blundering railway conductor mistook Liholiho for a black servant, and ordered him out of his railroad car. Liholiho recorded the event in his journal:

> Just because I had a darker skin than he had. Confounded fool. The first time I ever received such treatment, not in England or France, or anywhere else. But in this country I must be treated like a dog.... [34]

It was a bitter experience the future King Kamehameha IV would never forget.

The new King predicted an unhappy future for his Kingdom. Recalling David Malo's premonition, the King feared that American interests, particularly the missionary interests in Hawai'i

Dr. Gerrit Judd (l) with future Kings Kamehameha IV and V

would lead to the overthrow of the monarchy and annexation. The close call with annexation, as proposed by his uncle, Kamehameha III confirmed his suspicion.

Kamehameha IV felt prepared to handle the obligations of a monarch in a rapidly changing society. His travels to America and Europe with his brother Prince Lot and Dr. Gerrit Judd to negotiate treaties during 1849-1851, gave him the confidence to act rather than merely react to world events.

To sustain the sovereignty of his Kingdom, Kamehameha IV pursued a foreign policy to:

- Seek a treaty of reciprocity between the United States and Hawai'i, to allow Hawaiian sugar tax-free entry into the U.S.

- Establish friendly relations and get a satisfactory treaty with France

- Obtain a joint guarantee of Hawaiian independence from the world's great sea powers – Great Britain, France, the United States, and possibly Russia.[35]

Kamehameha IV earnestly sought a reciprocity treaty because both he and Hawaii's sugar growers believed that Hawaii's economy would improve if the U.S. eliminated its tax on imported Hawaiian sugar.

The 1850's were years of economic transition for Hawai'i. The once busy whaling industry – which saw up to 500 ships porting in Hawai'i annually – was declining, and the sugar industry was growing dramatically. By the 1860's, sugar had become Hawaii's primary export.

More than 125,000 acres of dry, barren land eventually would be irrigated and cultivated for sugar cane, Hawaii's only major crop that could be grown profitably on a large scale.[36]

The continued economic growth and prosperity of the sugar industry depended on tax-free entry into America. Hawaii's sugar growers failed to unify behind a single plan, and couldn't compete with Louisiana sugar growers. Some Hawai'i growers preferred eliminating American import taxes through annexation, while others supported a reciprocity treaty to allow the tax-free exchange of U.S. and Hawaiian goods.

The Hawaiian Government proposed a reciprocity treaty. Despite good intentions, the negotiated treaty failed to pass the U.S. Senate in 1855.

About the same time, a momentous international event made Hawaii's strategic mid-Pacific location more important than sandalwood or whaling or sugar: U.S. Commodore Matthew Perry succeeded in opening Japan to Western trade – ending Japan's 200 years of self-imposed isolation to the western world.

The resulting U.S.-Japan treaty signaled the beginning of America's active role in Asia. Every American ship traveling to Asia would now stop in Hawai'i.

Reciprocity or Annexation?

For the next 20 years, American and Hawaiian diplomats negotiated several reciprocity treaties. None succeeded in the U.S. Congress. American policy makers wanted more than sugar from Hawai'i. During negotiations for a reciprocity treaty, America expressed its desire for a military base and commercial harbor in Hawai'i.

Kamehameha IV preferred to reap the benefits of economic ties with the United States, not annexation.

What would America pursue: annexation or reciprocity?

To American leaders, reciprocity was intended as an interim or "second best solution" until annexation could be secured.

Now that America was settled on both coasts of the North American continent, expansionists asked, "where do we go now?" To those who envisioned the commercial and military importance of a mid-Pacific base, the answer was Hawai'i.

U.S. Secretary of State William Seward pursued a global vision for his nation by acquiring distant Alaska and the Midway Islands, obtaining the right to build a canal across Nicaragua, and making efforts to purchase from Denmark what is now called the U.S. Virgin Islands. An early advocate of annexation, Seward considered himself a skillful politician and persistent diplomat.

In 1864, Seward received a message from James McBryde, America's resident Minister in Hawai'i and a Kaua'i sugar plantation owner, asking why America should pay rent for Pearl Harbor when the property can be acquired:

> ...that if a reciprocity treaty at any time be made with this Government a fee simple (ownership) to a piece of land at this port (Pearl Harbor)...would be made one of the conditions of this treaty....[37]

Three years later, in 1867, Seward extended America's borders by purchasing giant-sized Alaska from Russia for $7 million.

Americans laughed, calling icy Alaska "Seward's folly," because the costly huge territory was too distant from the lower states.

Seward's eyes were on Hawai'i, too. However, the uproar that followed his Alaskan purchase, prevented him from seriously trying to obtain Hawai'i. Instead, Seward pursued an economic treaty with Hawai'i, not a political one.

In the autumn of 1866, U.S. Minister to Hawai'i Edward McCook astutely pointed out Hawaii's internal military and financial weaknesses in a letter to Secretary of State Seward:

> Geographically, these islands...(are) absolutely necessary to the United States. Destitute of both army and navy, the Hawaiian Government is without the power to resist aggression, to compel belligerants [sic] to respect the neutrality of her ports. Equally destitute of financial resources, they are without the means of indemnifying those who may suffer through their weaknesses.[38]

The reciprocity treaty that Seward proposed would have given America increased commercial benefits over the treaty that had been negotiated and defeated a decade earlier. Seward felt reciprocity was the first step to annexation, since new commercial advantages would bring Hawai'i politically closer to the United States.

In May, 1867, U.S. Minister Edward McCook suggested to Seward that a reciprocity treaty would "...prove the initial step toward the acquisition of the islands should this country ever want them."[39]

Seward agreed. His reply to McCook reveals his farsighted thinking:

> When the Pacific railroad is completed and the commerce of Asia directed to our Pacific ports, then these islands will be needed as a rendezvous for our Pacific navy, and a resort for merchant ships, and this treaty will have prepared the way for their quiet absorption.[40]

Seward, who preferred annexation over a reciprocity treaty, believed many Americans in Hawai'i also favored annexation. He sent this confidential message in September 1867, instructing U.S. Minister Edward McCook to determine if native Hawaiians supported annexation:

> ...A lawful and peaceful annexation of the islands to the United States with the consent of the people of the Sandwich Islands is deemed desirable by this Government and if the policy of annexation should really conflict with the policy of reciprocity, annexation is in every case preferred.[41]

In that same letter, Seward declared that those who desire "annexation of the Sandwich Islands, will be active in opposing a ratification of the reciprocity treaty."[42]

Seward was right. The reciprocity treaty was defeated because enough Senators viewed the treaty as an obstacle to annexation. On the other hand, some Senators objected to America's desire to control Hawaii's destiny.

The treaty actually received a majority vote in 1869 (24-22) and in 1871 (20-19), but a two-thirds vote was required for ratification.

U.S. Senator William Fessanden (R-Maine) arrogantly summarized annexation sentiment in 1868 when he said:

> ...it is folly to pay for a thing we already have...that the power and the prestige of the United States is sufficient to assure the concession of whatever naval and commercial privileges are needed in the islands....[43]

An interesting episode of this annexation effort involved a secret mission of Zephaniah Spalding, who came to Hawai'i in 1868, posing as a would-be cotton planter. U.S. Secretary of State William Seward sent Spalding to Hawai'i to report on the probable effect of a reciprocity treaty. Spalding's reports were sent as letters to his father, Congressman Rufus Spalding (R-Ohio), who forwarded the letters to the State Department.

A year later, Spalding wrote to his father that Americans in Hawai'i supported annexation, and believed the reciprocity treaty was hopeless. Speaking of annexation, the young Spalding declared: "It is time to decide upon the plan of action."[44]

Spalding, like Seward, advocated annexation, and urged the American Government to support the annexationists in Hawai'i. In a remarkably blunt letter which predicted events that would occur 25 years later, he declared that Americans in Hawai'i wanted the U.S. Government and its military to support their separatist cause:

> What they want is to know that they will be backed up by the United States and its representatives here in all proper measures taken by them to secure a change in the political sentiment of the islands and their annexation at the earliest possible period.

> This means not necessarily a war on the part of the United States, but a feeling that they are supported by our government and its officials, even to the continued presence of a man-of-war, if necessary, and intervention...

> Americans...claim that they have never had from the Government of the United States that...support England and France have always extended to their subjects here.

> If the United States should take possession tomorrow, on the ground that this (Hawaiian) Government has failed to respect American interests...I think it would hardly raise a single remonstrance either here or abroad. The feeling of foreigners seems generally to be that of astonishment to see the United States 'put up' with so much from this little Kingdom.[45]

Spalding felt annexation would be more quickly achieved if the reciprocity treaty were defeated.

Later that year, President Andrew Johnson urged Congress to approve a reciprocity treaty "until the people of these islands shall of themselves, at no distant day, voluntarily apply for admission into the Union."[46] President Johnson told Congress:

> It is known and felt by the Hawaiian Government and people that their government and institutions are feeble and precarious; that the United States being so near a neighbor, would be unwilling to see the islands pass under foreign control.[47]

Despite the President's encouragement, Congress approved neither annexation nor a reciprocity treaty.

A year later, President Johnson appointed annexation advocate Henry Peirce as U.S. Minister to Hawai'i, a Boston man with economic ties to the islands. Peirce had profited as a Honolulu merchant in the 1830's and visited the islands again in 1849, when he, Judge Lee and Bernice Pauahi's husband, Charles Bishop established what became known as Līhu'e Plantation. Peirce would serve eight years as U.S. Minister.

Peirce confidently told U.S. Secretary of State Hamilton Fish in a confidential message of February 25, 1871 that annexation is "the political destiny of this archipelago (which) seems a forgone conclusion."[48]

Two years later, U.S. Secretary of State Fish encouraged Peirce to pursue annexation:

> There seems to be a strong desire on the part of many persons in the islands, representing large interests and great wealth, to become annexed to the United States...There are also those of influence and of wise foresight who see a future that must extend the jurisdiction and the limits of this nation, and that will require a

resting spot in the mid-ocean, between the Pacific coast and the vast domains of Asia, which are now opening to commerce and Christian civilization...Should occasion offer, you will, without committing the government to any line of policy, not discourage the feeling which may exist in favor of annexation to the United States.[49]

Hawaiian Population Decline
Encourages Annexation

Throughout the 1800's, each succeeding generation of native Hawaiians declined by one-half. Overall, the native Hawaiian population decreased about 90% – from approximately 300,000 (recent estimates suggest the population was 800,000) in the days of Captain Cook to just 29,000 population in 1900.

By mid-century, people were predicting the extinction of the Hawaiian race. An 1850 Polynesian newspaper calculated that there would be less than 100 Hawaiians alive in the year 1930.[50] Fortunately, the population decline stabilized unexpectedly as the century ended.

Native Hawaiians, landless and poor after the Great Mahele, lacking immunity to foreign illness and disease, succumbed to: whooping cough, measles, mumps, cholera, influenza, smallpox, and colds.

To compound the population decline, thousands of native Hawaiians sought travel and adventure in distant shores. For many years, an average of 3,000 native Hawaiians departed annually on foreign whaling vessels and other trading ships.[51] In 1850, some 4,000 native Hawaiians joined whaling ships as seamen – one-eighth of the adult native Hawaiian population.[52] Few returned.

Each succeeding monarch suffered the burdens of witnessing the death of living and future generations of native Hawaiians.

After Kamehameha I, no surviving children were born to Hawaii's monarchs. Kamehameha II died in England at age 27,

after ruling five years.
Kamehameha III ruled for 30
years, but died at age 41 without any surviving children.
Kamehameha IV who died at
age 29, had one child, Prince
Albert, who died at age 4.

King Kamehameha IV and
Queen Emma worried about
the seemingly eventual extinction of the Hawaiian race. The
royal couple experienced a
tragic personal loss with the
sudden death of Prince Albert,
the last child born to the
Kamehameha family.

Prince Albert

Queen's Hospital, founded
by the royal couple to provide
free medical care for needy Hawaiians, stands as living testimony
to their everlasting concern for their people.

The rapid decline of the native Hawaiian population pro-
foundly influenced American foreign policy. In September,
1863, U.S. Minister to Hawai'i James McBryde informed Secretary of State William Seward:

> The native population is decreasing so rapidly as to
> produce the general, if not universal belief that within a
> short period, say from 20-40 years, there will be not enough
> of them remaining to perpetuate this government. This
> being the case, these islands must, of necessity, pass into
> other hands and their destiny controlled by other people.
> The question then is, to what nation shall they belong, and
> to whom ought they belong, the English or the Americans?
> They are our only competitors.[53]

Two months later, Kamehameha IV died of asthma and a grief-stricken heart on November 30, 1863. His older brother, Prince Lot reigned as Kamehameha V. Each brother reigned for nine years.

The royal line that began with Kamehameha the Great, ended with Kamehameha V.

Almost two years before the death of the last Kamehameha, U.S. Minister Henry Peirce reported to U.S. Secretary of State Hamilton Fish that he expected the bachelor King's eventual death would require the Legislature to elect a new monarch. Peirce

King Kamehameha V

believed this would produce "a crisis in political affairs," that would lead to a "propitious occasion to inaugurate measures for annexation of the islands to the United States...through means proper, peaceful, and honorable."

Peirce's letter to Fish was remarkably similar to the above-quoted McBryde letter of eight years earlier:

> The native population is fast disappearing; the number existing is now estimated at 45,000, having decreased about 15,000 since the census of 1866. The number of foreigners, in addition, is between 5,000 and 6,000, two-thirds of whom are from the United States, and they own a disproportionate share of wealth in Hawai'i.

Peirce asked: "To what foreign nation shall these islands belong if not to the great Republic?"[54]

Declining Native Hawaiian Population
1778-1900

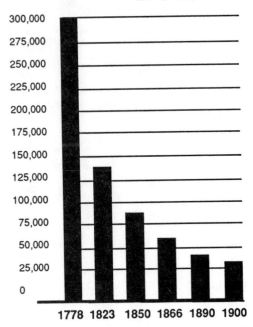

Source: Native Hawaiians Study Commission, Vol. I, p. 87-88

Immigration of Major Ethnic Groups
Primarily as Plantation Workers (1855-1899)

Year	Chinese	Japanese	Portuguese	Other	Total
1855-74	2,103	148		223	2,474
1875-79	8,107		599	692	9,398
1880-84	15,305		8,872	3,274	27,451
1885-89	3,262	10,600	1,088	46	14,996
1890-94	1,987	20,396	367		22,750
1895-99	7,368	32,273		613	40,254
total	38,132	63,417	10,926	4,848	117,323

Source: Linda Menton and Eileen Tamura, A History of Hawai'i (Honolulu: University of Hawai'i, 1989), p. 105.

Would it be America or England or France? Kamehameha V trusted the United States more than other nations.

Kamehameha V favored a strong independent monarchy, free from the Privy Council and the kuhina nui (premier), so he proclaimed a new constitution in 1864 after refusing an oath to uphold the existing missionary-inspired constitution.

Kamehameha V died without heirs, at age 43 in 1872. On his death bed, he asked High Chiefess Bernice Pauahi (Mrs. Charles Bishop) to succeed him. She declined.

The Hawaiian Constitution provided that the Legislature would choose a new monarch. A non-binding popular vote gave a large majority to Lunalilo, a cousin of Kamehameha V. The Legislature confirmed the victory against David Kalākaua, an attorney.

Lunalilo's reign was the shortest of any Hawaiian monarch. He died in 1874 at age 39, after one year as King.

To Americans living in Hawai'i and to America's leaders at home, the decline of the Hawaiian race contributed to the feeling that American control of Hawai'i was inevitable. The notion that another nation might control Hawai'i pushed America to desire Hawai'i even more. Population decline was one of several reasons for America's interest in annexation. Yet, despite the American influence in the Kingdom, the Americans were out-numbered by Europeans.

By 1890, U.S. Minister to Hawai'i John Stevens informed U.S. Secretary of State James Blaine in a confidential March 20 letter, that "the native population of 60 years ago is reduced to less than one-third...and it is continually growing less." He pointed out: "just one-half of the total population is of the original Hawaiian race...a small proportion of the lands and other proper-ties are in their possession."[55]

Acknowledging that 40% of the population was Chinese and Japanese, Stevens posed this rhetorical question: "shall Asiatic or American civilization ultimately prevail here?"[56]

America Spies on Pearl Harbor

By the 1870's, the prospering sugar industry brought benefits to Hawaii's economy, while also making the Kingdom's economy more dependent upon the United States. When a financial depression hit both Hawai'i and the United States in 1872, the need for a reciprocity treaty became increasingly important to Hawai'i sugar planters.

Annexation discussions emerged again.

U.S. Minister to Hawai'i Peirce informed U.S. Secretary of State Fish not to expect the Hawaiian Government to recommend annexation. He declared in early 1873 that annexation would be achieved only if:

> ...the planters, merchants, and foreigners...will induce
> the people to overthrow the (Hawaiian) Government, es-

Bernice Pauahi Bishop   **King Lunalilo**

tablish a republic, and then ask the United States for admittance into its Union.[57]

Instead of pursuing annexation, the King and Legislature submitted a new reciprocity treaty to the U.S. which gave Pearl Harbor to America. Some of the King's advisors felt this would improve the chances of winning a treaty. However, the native Hawaiian people objected, and the Pearl Harbor idea was withdrawn.

The proposal wasn't forgotten. The United States wanted Pearl Harbor.

U.S. Secretary of War W. Belknap sent military spies to survey and map Pearl Harbor, and to evaluate its military and commercial advantages.

On January 15, 1873, Major General John Schofield, commander of the United States Army Military Division of the Pacific, and Brigadier General B.S. Alexander of the Corps of Engineers, arrived in Honolulu, supposedly on a two month vacation trip. They were spies, under orders to report about:

> ...the defense capabilities of their different ports and their commerce facilities, and to examine into any other subjects that may occur to you as desirable, in order to collect all information that would be of service to the Country in the event of war with a powerful maritime nation...[58]

> It is believed the objects of this visit to the Sandwich Islands will be best accomplished if your visit be regarded as a pleasure excursion which may be joined in by your citizen friends....[59]

The Schofield and Alexander report stressed the significance of Pearl Harbor for naval and commercial purposes, and suggested that Hawai'i should give Pearl River to the United States in exchange for a reciprocity treaty. They noted that the Hawaiian Government:

...seem(s) fully alive to the necessity of relieving their principal independence from the heavy burden under which it now suffers, and no other mode of relief seems possible but annexation or reciprocity.[60]

General John Schofield

As the secret report was being prepared, U.S. Minister Peirce informed Secretary of State Hamilton Fish that Pearl Harbor is "sufficiently spacious" to provide safety for several hundred ships. [61]

For nearly 25 years, Schofield and Alexander's spy mission and their secret report were kept from the American public and the people of Hawai'i. The report was finally declassified in 1897 to support annexation in Congress.

Schofield served many years in influential policy making positions, including a brief stint as Secretary of War in 1868, and as Commanding General of the U.S. Army from 1888-1895. The U.S. military honored General Schofield by naming Schofield Barracks on O'ahu after him.[62]

Reciprocity Treaty Achieved

In February 1874, after barely a year on the throne, King Lunalilo died of tuberculosis, without an heir. Once again, the Legislature was obligated to choose a King. Again, David Kalākaua stepped forward as a candidate.

Kalākaua presented an easy-going personality, making him the kind of political leader who wanted to please everyone, but ended-up satisfying few, and hurting himself.

For now, Kalākaua was the right man at the right time, as far as Hawaiian sugar growers were concerned. Fearing economic ruin and desperate for a reciprocity treaty, the growers met secretly with Kalākaua, and struck a deal. The planters offered money and influence if Kalākaua would allow them to name his Cabinet officers. Kalākaua pledged to go to Washington to lobby for a reciprocity treaty, and the sugar planters agreed not to support giving the Pearl River to the United States.

Kalākaua knew that Hawaii's struggling economy needed the tax revenue that a profitable sugar industry would provide. He didn't need the sugar growers to convince him of that.

In the subsequent election, Kalākaua emerged victorious from this backroom political agreement, defeating Queen Emma, the widow of Kamehameha IV. Kalākaua hoped his alliance with the sugar planters would strengthen his rule.

When the Legislature confirmed Kalākaua's victory by a 39-6 vote, rioting broke out among Queen Emma's "Hawai'i for Hawaiians" supporters who accused native Hawaiian legislators of trading their votes for bribes. The new King stopped the riot with the aid of 150 American and 70 British soldiers who patrolled Honolulu's streets for eight days.[63]

Kalākaua fulfilled his promise to the sugar planters. In 1874, he made an unprecedented visit to Washington, urging President Ulysses Grant and the Congress to support the reciprocity treaty. Kalākaua was the world's first king to visit the United States.

A year later, the U.S. Senate ratified the treaty, but not without fateful consequences for Kalākaua.

To win Senate ratification of this economic treaty, supporters granted political considerations "that would give the U.S. a firm hold over the Isles."[64]

When the treaty reached the Senate floor, Senators discussed it behind the closed doors of a secret session. Secretary of State Hamilton Fish inserted a special clause into the treaty prohibiting any nation from leasing or obtaining Pearl Harbor. If the U.S. couldn't get Pearl Harbor, no other nation would. The clause read:

> It is agreed, on the part of his Hawaiian Majesty, that
> so long as this treaty shall remain in force he will not lease
> or otherwise dispose of or create any lien upon any port,
> harbor, or other territory in his dominions, or grant any
> special privilege or rights of use therein, to any other
> power....[65]

The treaty passed the Senate, 50-12. Since the treaty involved revenues, it was referred to the House of Representatives, where the Ways and Means Committee acknowledged that treaty ratification was influenced by fears that Great Britain would annex Hawai'i.

When the treaty was returned to the Senate to concur with House amendments, Senator Aaron Sargent (R-California) urged a novel but practical approach to annexation:

> The effect of the treaty is to encourage Americans to go
> there and make it (Hawai'i) an American colony...(I)t will
> cost us nothing to buy it...because it will be in our posses-
> sion as Texas was in our possession by the American
> population supplanting in influence and in numbers the
> Mexicans or Spaniards, by this influence which follows the
> trade and inducements to go there, making it an American
> colony.[66]

Many people in America envisioned Hawai'i as a gateway to the Pacific. America didn't want anyone else to have Pearl Harbor, the commercial key to the Pacific gateway.

And what did Hawaii's King think of this?

Kalākaua said he wasn't aware of the Pearl Harbor clause. Kalākaua's diplomatic representatives in Washington must have known about it, but it is not known if they informed King Kalākaua about it.

After the United States approved the treaty, British Minister James Wodehouse complained to Kalākaua about America's exclusive rights to Pearl Harbor. [67]

Despite the King's official objections to the Pearl Harbor clause, Kalākaua signed the treaty, which took effect in 1876.

Kalākaua received credit for his personal efforts to win a long-sought Reciprocity Treaty with the United States.

The Reciprocity Treaty benefited both nations. It allowed unrefined sugar, rice and almost all other Hawaiian products to be admitted to the United States tax free. In return, a long list of American products and manufactured goods would be shipped tax-free to Hawai'i.

Just a year later, U.S. Minister Peirce boasted that the Hawaiian Islands were "an American colony in all their material and political interests."[68]

For Hawaiian sugar growers, the treaty produced sweet profits. Sugar exports increased 10-fold, from 25 million pounds exported in 1875, to 250 million pounds in 1890.

The growth of Hawaii's sugar industry also led to massive irrigation projects, large financial ventures, centralized plantations (i.e., the large plantations bought the small ones), and the need for cheap, contract labor. From 1877-1890, more than 55,000 immigrant laborers were brought to Hawai'i, primarily from China, Japan, and Portugal.

On the other hand, the Reciprocity Treaty denied Hawai'i from offering comparably favorable treatment to any other nation.

The most significant outcome of the Reciprocity Treaty was the development of powerful economic ties between Hawai'i and the United States – setting in motion a series of events that would bring about fatal political consequences for Kalākaua, and ultimately, for the Hawaiian Kingdom.

The Reciprocity Treaty proved to be a turning point in what would lead to America's eventual control of Hawai'i.

In her autobiography, Lili'uokalani criticized the treaty for "put(ting) in peril the independence of our nation."[69] She was right. There was no turning back from the political consequences of this economic alliance.

European Imperialism and U.S. Manifest Destiny

"Hawai'i is a part of the productive and commercial system of the American States."
—U.S. Secretary of State James Blaine

European Imperialism

To obtain cheap labor and natural resources for industrialization, European nations extended their domain by conquering hundreds of weaker nations from the late 1800's until the early years of the 1900's.

In Africa, Asia, and in the Pacific region, England added five million square miles of new territory with 88 million people, while France added more than three million square miles with 37 million people.[1]

England, France, and Germany built empires from smaller and weaker Pacific islands, which they colonized and controlled militarily, economically, and culturally. The missionaries usually came first, followed by soldiers, merchants, planters, and other settlers.

By the late 1800's, large European and American navies were patrolling the huge Pacific Ocean.

What Europe and America wanted from the Pacific was its mineral resources, rubber, fibers, fertilizers from guano bird droppings, copra for soap and oils, a variety of foods (sugar, coffee, cocoa, vanilla, bananas, and various citrus fruits), and naval harbors.

As a result of these colonizing intrusions, hundreds of thousands of Pacific Islanders died from the white man's diseases, alcohol, or genocide. The natives and aborigines were not immune to foreign diseases or to foreign cannons and bullets.

Europe's imperialistic impulses were aided by the completion of the Suez Canal in 1869, which substantially shortened the time and distance from Europe to the newly acquired trade interests in Asia and the Pacific.

In the competitive desire for world trade and the political conquest of new territory, every imperialistic nation would protect its own interests.

Four nations were predominant in colonizing the Pacific Islands: Great Britain, France, Germany, and later, the United States.[2]

Great Britain:

- Australia
- New Zealand
- Fiji
- Rotuma
- New Hebrides
- Papua
- Christmas Island
- Cook Islands
- Niue
- Solomon Islands
- Ellice Islands
- Tonga
- Gilbert Islands (Kiribati)
- Ocean Island

France:

- Marquesas
- Tahiti
- New Caledonia
- Tuamotu Islands
- Wallis Island
- Maiao

Germany:

- N.E. New Guinea
- Bismarck Archipelago
- Marshall Islands
- bought Carolinas
- bought Marianas (except Guam)
- Western Samoa
- Solomon Islands

United States:	United States Naval Bases:
• Alaska	
• Midway Islands	• Wake Island
• Hawai'i	• Johnston Island
• Puerto Rico	• Midway Island
• Guam	• Hawai'i
• Philippines	• American Samoa
• Wake Island	• Guam
• East Samoa	

America's Manifest Destiny

Throughout the 19th Century, America expanded rapidly – in population, in geographic size, and in economic strength.

For example, America's size doubled in 1803 with the Louisiana Purchase, followed by acquisitions reaching Canada, Mexico, and the Pacific Ocean. Millions of immigrants flocked to America, contributing to a doubling of the U.S. population every 25 years, growing to 76 million people by 1900.

America prospered through industrialization with the discovery of minerals, the building of factories and mills, and the farming of fertile soil. This prosperity paralleled America's influence in world affairs.

Before the transcontinental railroad or the Panama Canal, America's growing West Coast population obtained its supplies more speedily from Hawai'i than from the U.S. East Coast.

Manifest Destiny During Mid-Century

About mid-century, American expansion inspired the self-confident belief that it was "manifest destiny," a phrase coined in 1845, to populate the continent and to become a great nation. U.S. President James Polk (1845-1849), an expansionist, incited the

Mexican-American War in order to obtain new territories for the expanding American nation.

President James Polk pursued a manifest destiny policy which: admitted Texas as the 28th state in 1845; fought and won the Mexican-American War, 1846-1848; and sought to obtain California and Oregon.

Just two years after gold was discovered in California in 1848, the "Golden State" was admitted to the Union as the 29th state in 1850; parts of Arizona and New Mexico were purchased in 1853; and Oregon was admitted as the 30th state in 1859.

As early as 1851, Congress passed a resolution asking the U.S. Navy and War Departments to report on how America's coastal areas would be defended in case of war. U.S. Naval Commander DuPont submitted a report which tied Hawai'i to America's future military needs:

> ...It is impossible not to estimate too highly the value and importance of the Sandwich Islands whether in a commercial or military point of view. Should circumstances ever place them in our hands, they would prove the most important acquisition we could make in the whole Pacific Ocean – an acquisition intimately connected with our commercial and naval supremacy in those seas...Those islands should never be permitted to pass into the possession of any European power....[3]

Manifest Destiny at the End of the 19th Century

During the last third of the 19th Century, the American military spied on Pearl Harbor and sent diplomatic spies to learn about annexation sentiment in Hawai'i. American policy makers in Washington and the diplomatic leaders who represented them in Hawai'i wrote boldly and often about annexation in their confidential reports. Sometimes they justified annexation on grounds of political and economic necessity, and sometimes they declared annexation was America's destiny.

Unlike the 1840's, manifest destiny now meant Pacific expansion and the annexation of Hawai'i. At the very least, Americans should prevent the Islands from falling into the hands of Great Britain, France, or Japan.

Despite the turmoil of the Civil War and Reconstruction Era of the 1860's, the ambitious Secretary of State William Seward pursued a global vision for America.

Seward directed the annexation of Midway Island in the Pacific, bought Alaska, acquired the right of transit across Nicaragua for a future Atlantic-Pacific canal, and negotiated a treaty to buy what's now called the Virgin Islands from Denmark. He also invoked the Monroe Doctrine to remove the French from Mexico and the Spanish from Santo Domingo.[4]

Like Seward before him, Secretary of State James Blaine advanced American interests in the international arena, as he laid the cornerstone for America's end-of-the-century manifest destiny policy.

Blaine's desires to annex Hawai'i are best summed-up in two letters – one confidential – dated December 1, 1881 to U.S. Minister James Comly in Hawai'i. Blaine's letters advocated American colonization of Hawai'i and emphasized imperialistic themes.

First he called attention to America's huge interest in the Pacific, extending all the way to Asia and Australia. Then Blaine speculated that the United States wouldn't hesitate to annex Hawai'i, if it were necessitated by a usurping foreign power.

According to Blaine, America's West Coast population and trade with Hawai'i had doubled in the brief five years since the Reciprocity Treaty went into effect, making Hawai'i "practically a part of the American system without derogation of their absolute independence."

As part of his global view, Blaine said: "It is not easy to set a limit to (America's) commercial activity or to foresee a check to

Profile: James Blaine

For nearly two decades, James Blaine led the Republican Party, having been Speaker of the U.S. House of Representatives, a U.S. Senator, a Secretary of State and a presidential aspirant. Blaine possessed the confidence of a "man of action," although his reputation suffered from questionable business ethics.[5]

A journalist by profession, he owned a small but influential weekly Maine newspaper, the *Kennebec Journal.*

Blaine served three Republican Presidents – James Garfield, Chester Arthur and Benjamin Harrison – as U.S. Secretary of State in 1881 and 1889-1892, a position which made him responsible for establishing and carrying out American policy toward Hawai'i.

Blaine almost became President in 1884. He lost a very close general election to Grover Cleveland, a Democrat, by just 62,000 votes out of more than 10 million votes cast, with a close electoral college vote, 219-182.

Four years later, Benjamin Harrison defeated Cleveland, and Blaine returned as Secretary of State from 1889 until mid-1892. In 1889, Blaine appointed his friend, John Stevens as U.S. Minister to Hawai'i. In 1893 Stevens conspired to overthrow the Queen and encourage annexation.

(America's) maritime supremacy in the waters of the Orient...."

Hawai'i fit conveniently into America's global plans. Blaine told Comly: "The United States has acquired a legitimately dominant influence in the North Pacific...The interests of Hawai'i must inevitably turn toward the United States in the future...as its natural and sole ally...."

This is a "logical recognition," Blaine added, "of the needs of

Hawai'i as a member of the American system of States rather than as a blind desire for a protectorate or ultimate annexation to the American Union...Hawai'i...is the key to the maritime dominion of the Pacific states...."

Blaine described America's "true and necessary policy of the Pacific":

> The Hawaiian Islands can not be joined to the Asiatic system. If they drift from their independent station it must be toward assimilation and identification with the American system, to which they belong by the operation of natural laws and must belong by the operation of political necessity.

He supported the "benevolent neutrality" of Hawai'i. However, if that is "impracticable, this Government would then unhesitatingly meet the altered situation by seeking an avowedly American solution for the grave issues presented."

Blaine added:

> ...Hawai'i is a part of the productive and commercial system of the American States. So far as the staple growths and imports of the islands go, the reciprocity treaty makes them practically members of an American zollverein, an outlying district of the State of California...

Blaine encouraged "a purely American form of colonization..." in Hawai'i. He advised U.S. Minister Comly:

> It will also be well for you in conversation with the leading men of Hawai'i to turn their thoughts discreetly in the direction of inviting American colonization there. A Hawaiian homestead act for the benefit of actual American settlers, with remission of taxation...might be in turn supplemented in the United States by voluntarily organized emigration schemes and cooperative aid to bona fide settlers.

Throughout the continent, north and south, where ever a foothold is found for American enterprise, it is quickly occupied, and this spirit of adventure, which seeks its outlet in the mines of South America and the railroads of Mexico, would not be slow to avail itself of openings for assured and profitable enterprise even in mid-ocean.

In that same letter, Blaine displayed a streak of smug racial superiority to explain the decreasing native Hawaiian population:

...The decline of the native Hawaiian element in the presence of newer and sturdier growths must be accepted as an inevitable fact, in view of the teachings of ethnological history...The problem of replenishment of the vital forces of Hawai'i presents itself for intelligent solution in an American sense − not in an Asiatic or British sense....

Here, Blaine revealed a desire to pursue annexation:

...Thirty years ago, having the choice between material annexation and commercial assimilation of the Islands, the United States chose the less responsible alternative. The soundness of the choice, however, evidently depends on the perpetuity of the rule of the native race as an independent government, and that imperiled, the whole framework of our relations in Hawai'i is changed, if not destroyed....[6]

Expansionist Secretary of State James Blaine wanted to annex Hawai'i, so he appointed his close friend, John Stevens as U.S. Minister to Hawai'i who conspired to overthrow the Queen and encourage annexation.

Manifest destiny popularized the notion that America was a great nation, so America needed Hawai'i in order to become a greater nation. Hawai'i offered a uniquely important benefit: a strategic mid-Pacific location to promote and defend America's growing commercial and military interests.

Kalākaua: a Tragic King

"I have heard it remarked that no change would be
satisfactory unless it was one deposing the King, changing the constitution, and adopting a republican form of
government."
—U.S. Minister George Merrill

"Serious trouble, if not a revolution, is imminent, at
no distant day."
—Rear Admiral George Brown

Kalākaua's Legacy

The strength of the annexation movement in Hawai'i had as
much to do with America's pursuit of manifest destiny as it did
with King Kalākaua's abrupt decline from power.

The Caucasian community despised the King's efforts to
create a Polynesian Kingdom of Pacific nations, and to revive
native Hawaiian culture (e.g., music, sports, dance and geneal-
ogy). His ambitious trip around the world in 1881 made him the
world's first monarch to circumnavigate the globe. For this
accomplishment, American diplomats accused him of trying to
sell his nation.

Kalākaua enjoyed the pleasures of wearing the crown. He saw
European and Asian monarchs living a lavish lifestyle, but he
failed to recognize that corruption and abuses of power could not
be defended by divine right, a concept Americans never accepted.

One of the King's Ministers, William Armstrong, cited the
weaknesses of autocratic rule in Hawai'i:

> The kings of Hawai'i did not understand the nature of
> ministerial government as contrasted with kingly or per-
> sonal government. In their simple minds, if there was a

King, he should rule. The fiction of a kingly figurehead as it existed in Great Britain, which was essentially the rule of...the people, was...beyond their (Hawaiians') understanding.

Armstrong added:

King Kalākaua

The white subjects of King Kalākaua, though able to destroy the monarchy because they possessed the brains and wealth of his Kingdom, cordially assented, though the majority of them were Americans, to its rule, but insisted that it should be ministerial rule. By refusing to submit to (ministerial government), the King had already put his throne in great jeopardy....[1]

The Caucasians in Hawai'i eventually took advantage of Kalākaua and humiliated him by imposing a new constitution against his royal wishes.

The King's bitter enemy and Government Minister Lorrin Thurston charged that Kalākaua acted like a Dr. Jekyl and Mr. Hyde with a "dual personality": sometimes genial and charming, other times lacking in morals.[2]

Kalākaua might have been a successful King. He was an educated man with worldly interests, and sensitive to the needs of his people. He helped the sugar planters obtain a Reciprocity Treaty that produced financial benefits for both the planters and the Kingdom economy.

Kalākaua's decline can be traced to questionable financial and

King Kalākaua crowns himself at his 1883 Coronation

moral habits, and to his selection of controversial political advisors, such as American-born Walter Murray Gibson and Italian-born Celso Moreno.

Walter Murray Gibson, elected to the Hawaiian House of Representatives in 1878, and appointed as Premier of the Kingdom in 1882, offended American leaders. Gibson suggested that Great Britain and other nations might protect Hawaii's independence if they received the same tax-free benefits as did the United States. Then he urged Kalākaua to make Hawai'i the center of a Polynesian Kingdom. This offended everyone but the native Hawaiians.

Money was the main obstacle to Kalākaua's vision of creating a Polynesian Kingdom. For example, a legislative proposal for a $10 million loan to finance the King's embarrassingly small, and mostly volunteer army and navy, produced an uproar from the sugar planters.

One planter-legislator, Representative Castle, threatened: "As surely as you vote for this measure, you hasten the end of the King's rule. We taxpayers will express our resentment in a concrete manner."[3]

On several occasions, American and British diplomats scolded the King when they disapproved of his policies.

For example, when Kalākaua appointed an Italian immigrant, Celso Moreno as Minister of Foreign Affairs, it produced a hostile reaction from American, British and French diplomats. They judged Moreno as a slick-talking adventurer who would try to profit from imaginative and deceptive schemes.

U.S. Minister James Comly warned the King: "Unless Moreno is discharged, the diplomatic corps has agreed to ask their governments to send warships and intercede to protect the lives and property of their nationals."[4]

Reluctantly, Kalākaua dismissed Moreno, whose entire stay in the Kingdom was less than 10 months.

Once again, warship diplomacy succeeded in Hawai'i. Whether Moreno was qualified or not, the incident raised a constitutional issue that would emerge again. Did the King have the right to appoint and remove Cabinet ministers without interference from foreign diplomats?

American meddling continued.

Kalākaua's World Trip

In January, 1881, King Kalākaua completed a world trip, with visits to the United States, and most of the major capitols of Europe and Asia.

The purpose of the trip was to explore ways to encourage people from other countries to immigrate to Hawai'i to help reverse the population decline and to provide the necessary labor force for sugar plantations. Unfortunately, he also saw how lavishly many of his fellow monarchs lived, and he tried to emulate their lifestyle of grandeur.

While in Japan, Kalākaua laid the foundation for importing

tens of thousands of contract workers for the sugar plantations, who would soon comprise 40% of the Kingdom population.

Kalākaua also suggested that 5-year old Princess Kaʻiulani should someday marry the then 15-year old Japanese prince to establish a royal alliance among the two nations, and perhaps to discourage American efforts to dominate Hawaiʻi. However Japanese Emperor Meiji rejected the marriage alliance.[5]

U.S. Secretary of State James Blaine worried about Kalākaua's expedition. He feared rumors that the King's need for economic aid might tempt him to sell part of his Kingdom to a foreign country. To safeguard American interests, Blaine advised U.S. diplomats to observe the King's activities and to warn each government that the United States would not allow any land sale.

The rumor caught up with the King in Vienna. Kalākaua denied having intentions of selling the islands to any European government. On the contrary, he told newspaper reporters that the European powers should unify behind a guarantee of Hawaii's independence.

The *New York Times* editorialized:

> It is an open secret that Kalākaua, King of the Hawaiian Islands, is on a voyage around the world for the purpose of selling his Kingdom. If annexation ever arrives, it must take the islands to the United States.[6]

While visiting Italy, the King met his former minister, Moreno. The King's traveling companions, Charles Judd and William Armstrong, who accompanied the King at the insistence of the ever-watchful Sugar Planters' Association, discovered that Moreno was attempting "to secure from the European countries a guarantee of the perpetual independence of the Hawaiian Kingdom."[7]

Even after Kalākaua returned to Hawaiʻi, U.S. Secretary of State Blaine continued to express concern about a possible land sale. Blaine repeated a familiar theme in this letter to U.S. Minister James Comly:

The Government of the United States has always avowed and now repeats that, under no circumstances, will it permit the transfer of the territory or sovereignty of these Islands to any of the great European powers.[8]

Kalākaua never discussed a land sale on his tour. Instead, he admired the wealth and cultures of his hosts.

Kalākaua enjoyed reviewing the military troops of his host nations. Whenever he was asked about the size of his army or navy, he shied away, embarrassed to admit that he had but one small ship and a 75-man volunteer army for guarding the Palace and parading on holidays.

Armstrong, who chronicled the King's trip around the world and later became Kalākaua's Minister of Immigration, wrote: "We had hoped that the subject of our military establishment would be ignored." Whenever "it frequently and sorely confronted us" the King became "depressed in spirit."

In one instance, Armstrong told his Japanese hosts: "Your navy is our navy because you are interested in maintaining our independence." Armstrong also wrote:

As a nation, our independence was carefully protected by the jealousy of the European and American nations, so that for all practical purposes their navies were our navy, especially that of the United States.[9]

A Polynesian Empire?

Soon after Kalākaua returned to Hawai'i, the 1875 Reciprocity Treaty was nearing the end of its seven-year life. The Sugar Planters' Association sent a draft of a new treaty to William Green, Hawaii's Minister of Foreign Affairs, with a clause that Pearl River be ceded to the United States.

Green objected:

Beretania Street (1880's). Washington Place is on the right and the current State Capitol site is on the left

> I do not believe that the proposal is a sound one...The United States had made no demand for (Pearl River)...they wish only that no other power should control it and that is what we all want.[10]

Green's response infuriated the Sugar Planters' Association, which secretly decided to depose him. They succeeded. Green resigned, and the King appointed Gibson as Prime Minister.

The controversial Gibson quickly became Kalākaua's biggest liability.

Financial matters continued to plague the Hawaiian Government. Sugar planters complained that the government was spending too much money for Hawaiian cultural programs, while business interests took a back seat. Each appropriation brought renewed protests from the opposition.

Armstrong wrote that Kalākaua supported "any scheme that supplied him with large sums of money (that) would relieve him from dependence on (white people)."[11]

Armstrong also noted that Caucasians criticized Kalākaua for

King and Fort Streets (about 1885)

his "grand style of living," for crowning himself at a lavish ceremony, and especially for building the costly 'Iolani Palace. From 1880-1890, Hawaii's national debt increased from $390,000 to $2.6 million.[12]

Prime Minister Gibson enjoyed the friendship of sugar magnate Claus Spreckels, who tried – and failed – to ease Kalākaua's debt with a controversial $2 million loan in 1886. People worried that Spreckels would gain "dictatorial" financial control over the Kingdom.

As part of his plan to make Hawai'i the center of a Polynesian Kingdom, Kalākaua sent a delegation to Samoa in 1887 to establish a political confederation. This angered Germany, which was trying to colonize Samoa. German Chancellor Bismarck sent irate messages to Washington, demanding that Hawai'i not interfere. As a result, the U.S. State Department ordered Kalākaua to stop making the world powers angry.

The message here was: it was okay for Europe to colonize, but not for Hawai'i to establish its own sphere of influence or try to unify other Pacific nations for self-preservation.

The fact was, the Hawaiian Government had notified 26 Polynesian nations that they should govern themselves without fear of being annexed by any major world power. Kalākaua merely implemented a resolution approved by the Hawai'i Legislature in 1883 creating a Royal Hawaiian Commissioner to represent the Hawaiian Government to the peoples of Polynesia.

America Wants Hawai'i

America wanted to annex all of Hawai'i, not merely to obtain the exclusive use of Pearl Harbor.

The leaders of the Hawaiian Kingdom were divided over the possibility of losing Pearl Harbor as well as sovereignty to the United States. On the other hand, many of Hawaii's prominent merchants and planters who held dual Hawaiian-American citizenship supported ceding Pearl Harbor since they were financially-dependent on the sugar bounty.

Native Hawaiians resented the political and economic power wielded by the small, oligarchic-minded European and American population, which numbered less than 3,000 people prior to the immigration of Portuguese laborers for the sugar plantations.

The success of the Reciprocity Treaty tied Hawai'i to America and to American business interests.

William Irwin, a prominent British-born citizen of Hawai'i who prospered as a business associate of "sugar king" Claus Spreckels of California, recognized these economic interests when he told the *Pacific Commercial Advertiser* newspaper, that the Hawaiian Islands are:

> ...the key to the Pacific, and the United States should
> continue to control them. Nearly all important government
> positions are held by Americans, and the Islands are really
> an American colony.[13]

The U.S. Finally Gets Pearl Harbor

For many years, the American Government desired to obtain Pearl Harbor – perhaps as much for military and commercial purposes as to prevent another nation from obtaining it.

The proposed Reciprocity Treaty that President Grover Cleveland submitted to the U.S. Senate in 1884 emerged substantially different from the one approved by the Senate Foreign Relations Committee two years later, in 1886.

The amended treaty called for an American naval station near Honolulu, which most likely would be Pearl Harbor. The amendment was proposed by Senator John Morgan (D-Alabama), an expansionist Democrat, who would later play a prominent policy making role in Hawai'i affairs.

The full Senate failed to pass the treaty resolution until three events got their attention: Kingdom efforts to obtain a loan from England, a proposed reciprocity treaty with Canada, and a willingness to give away Pearl Harbor.

- In September, 1886, the Hawaiian Government, always short of cash, sought a $2 million loan from England. In return, Hawai'i pledged its public revenue as collateral security. Rumors of this loan aroused American anxieties about foreign influence in Hawai'i. The United States worried that such a loan would interfere with its preferred rights gained under the 1875 Reciprocity Treaty.

  U.S. Secretary of State Thomas Bayard explained to U.S. Minister to Hawai'i George Merrill in a confidential letter of January 8, 1887 that he viewed England's loan as "possible control by foreign creditors over the financial measures and administration of the Hawaiian Government."[14]

- Many Senators reacted uneasily to rumors that Hawai'i might negotiate a reciprocity treaty with Canada.

- Hawaiian sugar growers, desperate to renew the Reciprocity Treaty, seized the opportunity to make a deal. To win the treaty, the financially strapped Kingdom offered to give the United States a lease and exclusive control of Pearl Harbor for use as a naval base.

All of a sudden, the U.S. Senate was anxious to ratify the Reciprocity Treaty if it meant denying a European power a foothold in Hawai'i.

The U.S. Senate approved a renewed Reciprocity Treaty on January 20 giving the U.S. exclusive rights to use Pearl Harbor.

This pleased the King's Cabinet, but Kalākaua objected. Pressure from the powerful new Bayonet Cabinet was too great. When the Reform Party won control of the Hawai'i Legislature in special legislative elections that year, the new Cabinet notified Henry Carter, Hawaii's Minister to the U.S., that the King had consented (probably unwillingly) to the treaty and its Pearl Harbor amendment.[15]

At last, the United States finally acquired Pearl Harbor – nearly 30 years after the first diplomatic suggestion was made by U.S. Minister James McBryde to Secretary of State Seward in 1864, and 14 years after America's 1873 military spy mission which surveyed and mapped the future naval base.

Despite the setback, Kalākaua succeeded in complicating matters for the Americans by employing a clever legal maneuver suggested by Hawai'i diplomat Henry Carter. Kalākaua sent the U.S. Secretary of State a stipulation that the privilege for using Pearl Harbor should last only as long as the seven-year treaty. [16]

In other words, if Hawai'i chose to renounce the treaty sometime in the future, the U.S. might lose Pearl Harbor – or so the Americans feared.

Secret Hawaiian League Established

The year 1887 was pivotal to the events leading to the eventual overthrow of the Hawaiian monarchy. Not only did the Kingdom lose Pearl Harbor, but the King lost his authority to rule.

During the discussion for a new Reciprocity Treaty, a small but influential group of Caucasian businessmen and planters established a secret Hawaiian League and a political Reform Party which challenged King Kalākaua for power.

Kalākaua's reputation declined, both internationally and at home. Within Hawai'i, a group of so-called "reformers" – a mixture of Caucasian merchants who regarded themselves as a "morally righteous group" established the opposition political Reform Party. Native Hawaiians called them the "Missionary Party," because many, like Dole, Thurston, Smith, Judd, and Damon, were descendants of former missionaries.

At first, the Reform Party advocated better government, and supported a constitutional rather than an absolute monarchy. However, their brand of "reform" emphasized not the betterment of everyone's liberties and rights, but the promotion of Caucasian rights and the restriction of political rights enjoyed by native Hawaiians.

Some wanted to dethrone the King.

These "reformers" were stirred to action by Kalākaua's conduct – such as his attempts to create a Polynesian empire, and his financial abuses, including a bribery-scandal in which the King accepted a $75,000 "gift" in exchange for an opium license that another man received.

Reform Party members established a secret Hawaiian League in early 1887 with 405 members, led by a "Committee of 13".

Lorrin Thurston, a member of the Legislature, was a founder of the League, it's most energetic propagandizer, and a leading agitator for annexation.

The objective of the Hawaiian League, according to its constitution, was: "constitutional, representative government, in fact as well as in form...by all necessary means."[17]

Thurston said he was inspired to establish the Hawaiian League and later to dethrone the monarchy after reading about the

Profile: Lorrin Thurston

Lorrin Thurston, the grandson of Asa Thurston who came to Hawai'i with the first missionary company in 1820, was a fist-clenching, loud-talking firebrand who played a leading role in the Queen's dethronement and in U.S. annexation.

Lorrin Thurston received a law degree from Columbia University, worked part-time as editor of the *Honolulu Bulletin* newspaper in 1884, and served three years in the Bayonet Cabinet as Minister of the Interior.

Thurston and William Smith were partners in a small law office near the corner of Fort and Merchant Streets. However Thurston neglected his law practice for the politics of government and revolution.

He was elected to the House of Representatives in 1886 from Moloka'i and Lāna'i, and to the House of Nobles in 1892 from Maui.

Thurston established the secret Hawaiian League, wrote the 1887 Bayonet Constitution, wrote the 1893 proclamation which declared the monarchy vacant, and served as the Provisional Government's Minister to the U.S. for annexation. After 1900, he became principal owner and editorial director of the *Honolulu Advertiser*.

French revolutionaries who won their rights from the despotic King Louis XVI.[18]

Three years earlier, in an 1884 *Honolulu Daily Bulletin* newspaper editorial, Thurston explained that some people desired annexation for purposes of making money or political security. He said "the majority of intelligent foreigners, and especially those born here of foreign parents," encourage annexation for the best interests of the native Hawaiians.

Thurston wrote:

> ...It is certain that (the United States) Government will not permit its interests here to be sacrificed nor permit any other foreign government to control here. When these Islands cease to be self-governing the United States Government will take possession.[19]

The Bayonet Constitution

Irate with the political, economic and moral excesses of King Kalākaua and his Minister, Walter Murray Gibson, the Caucasian "reformers" and Hawaiian League members were anxious to exert political control. They ordered Kalākaua to remove Gibson, and demanded specific constitutional changes to weaken the King's power and authority.

The secret Hawaiian League gained the support of an all-Caucasian, military organization known as the Honolulu Rifles. This para-military organization was led by the militant-radical, Volney Ashford, whom Thurston described as "an evil genius" lacking in principles. Ashford, a Canadian lawyer who had lived in Hawai'i less than two years, proposed that all government office holders should be filled by Hawaiian League members.[20]

According to Thurston, Ashford wanted to have Kalākaua assassinated during a shooting contest, but the League rejected the suggestion.[21]

Like many activist organizations, the Hawaiian League was

Clarence Ashford (1888)   Volney Ashford

more divided than unified. The League attracted both radicals and conservatives, each with different goals.

Ashford said the movement "...embraced the establishment of an independent republic, with the view to ultimate annexation to the United States."[22]

In contrast, conservative Sanford Dole said the League "was not an annexation movement in any sense, but tended toward an independent republic...."[23]

Concerning the in-house fighting of League members, William R. Castle explained: "a very strong element" in the League was determined to achieve annexation.

Castle added that "those of Hawaiian birth, parentage and affiliation," received a promise from the entire League that any efforts would be confined to making the Hawaiian Government "responsible and safe."[24]

In its first years, the League's conservative members usually prevailed.

Despite the differences of Hawaiian League members, they unified behind one issue – race.

According to Z.S. Spalding, a League member with sugar interests, "reform" meant that "the rights of the white people would be more respected and observed."[25]

U.S. Minister George Merrill summarized Hawaii's intensifying internal problems in this report to Secretary of State Thomas Bayard:

> Public feeling has been intense against the King while the daily press has been outspoken in denouncing the King, the Ministry and nearly all officials throughout the Kingdom. Among the people, foreign residents especially, there has been aroused a feeling that a change must soon occur from the highest to lowest official...I have heard it remarked that no change would be satisfactory unless it was one deposing the King, changing the constitution and adopting a republican form of government.[26]

Soon afterwards, Merrill wrote that he had "quietly counseled (the Americans about) moderation and the adoption of peaceful measures as the best method of bringing about a proper administration of affairs."[27]

Trouble was brewing in the Kingdom. The Caucasians were anxious to gain political power.

Kalākaua asked U.S. Minister Merrill for advice, "unofficially, but as a friend, concerning the present political situation...."

Merrill reported to Washington on June 27, 1887:

> Since he (Kalākaua) had frankly asked my opinion, I thought it was better for many reasons to heed the voice of the people especially those who were paying the taxes, had accumulated wealth in the country....[28]

Three days later, the King's opponents held a public meeting.

Honolulu Rifles (1881)

Lorrin Thurston read some resolutions prepared by the Committee of 13 which included the commitment "to the policy of securing a new constitution,"[29] as well as calling for the dismissal of both Gibson and the entire Cabinet.

The Committee spent the next several days writing a new constitution with Lorrin Thurston as its chief author.

On the morning of July 6, Colonel Volney Ashford and the Honolulu Rifles seized a shipment of arms sent to Hawai'i from Australia, thinking it was intended for the King. Ashford then took a squad of the Honolulu Rifles to Gibson's home, arrested Gibson and threatened to hang him. Fortunately for Gibson, the Honolulu Rifles were dissuaded by the conservative members of the Hawaiian League.

The vigilante Honolulu Rifles and the Hawaiian League now ruled Honolulu.

To cope with this crisis, Kalākaua called a meeting of the

foreign diplomats that same day. According to U.S. Minister Merrill, Kalākaua said:

> Armed men were patrolling the streets, and not know-ing what the next act might be, he desired to place the control of the affairs of the Kingdom in our hands. This offer we informed him could not be accepted and it was the desire of all other powers that he should maintain himself in authority....[30]

After the meeting, Merrill reported that foreign diplomats "passed down to the central portion of the city, assured the people that the King had acceded to their request and was now forming a Ministry with Mr. Green as Premier and no necessity for further excitement existed."[31]

Merrill didn't identify the Hawaiian League by name, but that's who he spoke to. He told the Hawaiian League that Kalākaua had agreed to their resolutions for political "reform."

By late afternoon, the "reformers" handed the King a new constitution, and gave him 24 hours to sign it, which he did after a few hours of argument and discussion.

The King agreed to appoint a new Cabinet of these Hawaiian League members: W. L. Green, Godfrey Brown, Lorrin Thurston, and Clarence Ashford, the younger brother of Volney Ashford.

Merrill noted that all, except Thurston, were of British origin, and that the "principal American merchants...generally coincide in the opinion that the present Ministers are satisfactory, and favorable to the welfare of the Kingdom."[32]

Kalākaua didn't have much choice. That's why it's called the Bayonet Constitution.

Lorrin Thurston credited Kalākaua's decision to sign the Constitution with adherence to the adage: "He who fights and runs away may live to fight another day."[33]

Thurston accused then-Princess Liliʻuokalani of hoping Kalākaua would abdicate so she could reign.

Thurston wrote: "She stated publicly that she wished she had been 'wearing the pants'" when Kalākaua submitted to the new Constitution. According to Thurston, she accused Kalākaua of "cowardice." At the time, Princess Lili'uokalani was in London attending Queen Victoria's Golden Jubilee.[34]

On the other hand, Lili'uokalani said she knew of a plot to assassinate the King if he didn't sign the Bayonet Constitution.[35] Some native Hawaiians asked her to become monarch if Kalākaua abdicated.

The Bayonet Constitution gave control of the government to the Caucasian planters and businessmen by:

- reducing the King to a ceremonial leader
- eliminating most of the monarch's power
- prohibiting the monarch from dismissing a Cabinet member without approval from the Legislature
- requiring the monarch to sign all bills and resolutions (even those that he vetoed)
- establishing property and income requirements for voting and holding office
- requiring all voters to sign an oath supporting the 1887 Constitution
- excluding all people born in Asia from voting

In addition, the new Constitution required Kalākaua to name heirs to the throne, so he added Prince Kawānanakoa and Prince Jonah Kūhiō Kalaniana'ole.

Prior to 1887, the Cabinet was responsible to the King. The King appointed all 20 nobles, who would meet in the same legislative body with the 28 elected Representatives. Now, there would be an equal number of Nobles and Representatives, 24 each.

From now on – the Cabinet, not the monarch – would govern Hawai'i. Yet whichever political party controlled the Legislature would control the Cabinet. Native Hawaiians held a majority of the vote for the Representatives, but the Caucasians held a majority of the vote for the Nobles.

The Kingdom's new Attorney General, Clarence Ashford, defended the reformers' actions. He told the *New York Herald* newspaper:

> If the new Constitution had been submitted to the Legislature it would simply mean that at the end of two years the King would say 'This does not suit me' and (he would) kill it by absolute veto. There was only one way to proceed, and that was to arbitrarily force the King into giving us a better form of government.[36]

Native Hawaiians objected. Tension increased. Many feared violence.

Barely a week later, U.S. Secretary of State Thomas Bayard sent these precedent-setting instructions to U.S. Minister George Merrill:

> Your own aid and counsel, as well as the assistance of the officers of our government vessels, if found necessary, will...be promptly afforded to promote the reign of law and respect for orderly government in Hawai'i.[37]

This message gave the U.S. Minister authority to call out American troops if he thought American lives and property were threatened by violence.

Surprisingly, there was no eruption of violent protests by native Hawaiians to the Bayonet Constitution.

And in late September, Bayard notified Merrill that American citizens could take an oath to support the new Hawaiian Constitution, vote, and hold office without losing American citizenship.[38] The oath enabled several hundred more Americans and Europeans to vote. Prior to 1887, less than one-third of the foreigners were naturalized and eligible to vote.[39]

Many questioned the constitutionality of the Bayonet Constitution. Nearly 50 years later, its author, Lorrin Thurston wrote a typically uncompromising rebuttal in his memoirs:

> Unquestionably the constitution was not in accordance with law; neither was (America's) Declaration of Independence from Great Britain. Both were revolutionary documents which had to be forcibly effected and forcibly maintained.[40]

The royal legacy of King Kalākaua, the man who was elected King with the support of the sugar planters, had lost nearly all the privileges of a monarch. The Bayonet Constitution reduced Kalākaua to a mere figurehead of a king, with little power to do anything.

The well-organized Reform Party won the 1888 elections aided by the votes of foreigners, especially the contract labor Portuguese immigrants, who gained the vote by the new constitution.

Now in full control, the "reformers" repealed or enacted laws that further eroded the King's power.

Albert Judd, who served as Hawai'i Supreme Court Chief Justice from 1874-1900, recalled that the Caucasian-imposed 1887 Bayonet Constitution was "a successful revolutionary act."[41]

The Caucasian foreigners and so-called "reformers" succeeded in reducing the King's power, without dethroning the monarch...at least not yet.

In her autobiography, Lili'uokalani complained of the ingratitude of Hawaii's foreign residents:

> By his (Kalākaua's) investigations and solution of the problem of labor he gave them (American sugar planters) the opportunity to raise sugar at an enormous profit; and he thus devoted the earlier part of his reign to the aggrandizement of the very persons, who, as soon as they had become rich and powerful, forgot his generosity, and plotted a subversion of his authority, and an overthrow of the consti-

tution under which the Kingdom had been happily governed for nearly a quarter of a century.[42]

She continued:

For many years our sovereigns had welcomed the advice of, and given full representations in their government and councils to American residents who had cast in their lot with our people, and established industries on the Islands. As they became wealthy, and acquired titles to lands...their greed and their love of power proportionately increased...So the mercantile element, as embodied in the Chamber of Commerce, the sugar planters, and the proprietors of the missionary stores, formed a distinct political party...whose purpose was to minimize or entirely subvert other interests, and especially the prerogatives of the crown...If we manifested any incompetency, it was in not foreseeing that they would be bound by no obligations, by honor, or by oath of allegiance, should an opportunity arise for seizing our country, and bringing it under the authority of the United States.[43]

She added:

Is there another country where a man would be allowed to vote, to seek for office, to hold the most responsible of positions, without becoming naturalized, and reserving to himself the privilege of protection under the guns of a foreign man-of-war at any moment when he should quarrel with the government under which he lived? Yet this is exactly what the quasi-Americans, who call themselves Hawaiians now and Americans when it suits them, claimed the right to do at Honolulu.[44]

The Caucasians desired, Lili‘uokalani charged, "above all things the extension of their power...."[45]

The Wilcox Rebellion

Historian Ralph Kuykendall explained that the "reformers"
believed their Bayonet Constitution created a weak constitutional
monarchy they could live with:

> But the Hawaiian monarchy did not willingly accept
> the role assigned to it by the 1887 Constitution. It wanted
> the sovereign to be not merely a glamorous symbol of the
> power of the nation but the actual repository and wielder of
> that power as he had been in earlier years. The conflict
> between these two concepts of government is the most
> important feature of the history of the remaining years of
> the Kingdom.[46]

Was Kalākaua too submissive to the demands of the "reformers"? Many native Hawaiians suggested that Kalākaua should
give up his throne in favor of his sister, Princess Liliʻuokalani.

Publicly, Princess Liliʻuokalani told the King not to abdicate.
Privately, was she seeking the throne before her time?

Many native Hawaiians hoped to regain the right to vote and
hold legislative office that the foreigners took from them. Soon
after the Bayonet Constitution, native Hawaiians submitted resolutions asking for a return to the former constitution, that all
volunteer para-military companies be disbanded, and all guns and
ammunition be taken away from citizens. Later, some native
Hawaiians threatened violence and insurrection. They were
frustrated, and becoming hostile.

Finally, in 1889, two years after the forced adoption of the
Bayonet Constitution, Robert Wilcox led a led a group 100 mostly
native Hawaiians in a failed attempt to restore the King's constitutional rights. On July 30, 1889, while Kalākaua was safely
absent from ʻIolani Palace, Wilcox and his followers briefly
occupied the four-acre Palace grounds.

The insurrection was crushed the day it began, with the aid of

Profile: Robert Wilcox

Enter Robert Wilcox, a tall, slim part-Hawaiian with Maui royalty in his blood.

At the young age of 25, his leadership abilities attracted the attention of King Kalākaua. In 1880 Kalākaua sent Wilcox to Italy with Celso Moreno, where Wilcox and two other Hawaiian youths attended the Royal Military Academy and studied engineering.

The Cabinet of the Bayonet Constitution recalled Wilcox in 1887, probably to save the money being spent on his education. In the years ahead, Wilcox caused the "reformers" so much trouble, they probably regretted their decision to recall him, and they probably wished they'd spent money to keep him in Italy.

Wilcox, a magnetic speaker, excelled as a political agitator and attracted loyal followers.

He led two unsuccessful revolts against the Caucasian-imposed Bayonet Constitution and the Republic of Hawai'i, in 1889 and 1895. After the 1895 revolt, the Hawai'i Government sentenced Wilcox to death, then commuted his punishment to imprisonment. Later, he served as Hawaii's first Territorial Representative in the U.S. Congress, from 1900-1902.

Wilcox lost a re-election bid to another former political prisoner – the only Prince to survive a death sentence and serve in the U.S. Congress, Jonah Kūhiō Kalaniana'ole.

80 American soldiers. Six insurgents were killed. About 60 people were imprisoned.

Ironically, when native Hawaiians took arms to revoke the Bayonet Constitution, the U.S. Minister to Hawai'i George Merrill called in American troops "for the protection of people and property."[47] This lesson was not lost on the native Hawaiian people.

Wilcox was tried for his crime, but acquitted by a native Hawaiian judge. Young Wilcox will be heard from again.

His revolt signaled the beginning of nearly continuous political unrest in Hawai'i.

After the failed Wilcox revolt, the "reformers" pressed the King to surrender virtually all his power. They wanted to monopolize and control all the powers of government. A month later, on August 3, the new Cabinet informed Kalākaua that they would be "absolutely responsible" for running the government. They told Kalākaua:

> Your Majesty shall in the future sign all documents and do all acts which under the laws or the Constitution require the signature or act of the sovereign, when advised to do by the Cabinet....[48]

The weakened King protested all the way to the Hawai'i Supreme Court. Kalākaua lost there, too. The court issued this terse ruling:

> There can be no authority without responsibility. The King is without responsibility. The Constitution confers responsibility of the Government upon the Cabinet: They therefore have the authority.[49]

Things couldn't get worse for the Kingdom, could they? Yes, they could.

U.S. Secretary of State James Blaine appointed his good friend John Stevens as the new U.S. Minister to Hawai'i.

An avowed expansionist long before he arrived in Hawai'i on September 23, 1889, Stevens lost little time initiating a campaign to achieve annexation.

1890 Elections

Soon after the Wilcox revolt, Rear Admiral L.A. Kimberly sensed the possible outbreak of violence during the upcoming 1890 elections. Kimberly informed Secretary of Navy B.F. Tracy in October, 1889:

> The natives seem to have an uneasy feeling as to their rights being usurped by the whites, and their gradual loss of prestige and power in the Government...There is an agitation quietly working as to the race question, which no doubt will become a prominent factor....[50]

Kimberly asked Secretary of Navy Tracy for permission to dispatch American soldiers to preserve order and to protect the security of Americans "if necessity arises."[51]

The request for troops was approved by both Secretary of State Blaine and Secretary of Navy Tracy.[52]

By February, the day before the 1890 election, British Minister James Wodehouse predicted a violent election day uprising from native Hawaiians. He convinced U.S. Minister John Stevens to agree "that guards for the English and American Legations should be landed tomorrow morning from the English and American war ship now in the port."[53] However, the Kingdom Cabinet persuaded the two diplomats to cancel their plans.

The persuasive joint efforts of the American and British Ministers kept Kalākaua from endorsing a new constitution, even though it was a major campaign issue of the native Hawaiians.

Election day 1890 was peaceful, as two major political parties competed for votes:

Profile: John Stevens

John Stevens was born in 1820, the same year New England missionaries first arrived in Hawai'i.

Stevens became a pastor and leader of the Maine anti-slave movement, and a founder of the Maine Republican Party. He served in the Maine Legislature from 1865-1870.

After writing some articles for the small but nationally prominent *Kennebec Journal*

newspaper, owned and edited by James Blaine, Stevens and Blaine began a 38-year friendship. Stevens joined the newspaper as co-editor and publisher in 1855.

Coincidentally, the newspaper was founded by Luther Severance, who as U.S. Commissioner to Hawai'i during the 1850's, guided King Kamehameha III toward American annexation.

Stevens began his diplomatic career as Minister to Uruguay and Paraguay (1870-1874), then as Minister to Norway and Sweden (1877-1883).[54]

According to Helena Allen, biographer of Queen Lili'uokalani, Stevens had been removed from both posts as an American Minister after meddling in the internal affairs of each host nation.[55]

Stevens, like Blaine, sought to maintain American predominance in Hawai'i, and in the world. He worried about the influence of Britain, and a Japanese takeover of Hawai'i. These fears were more alarmist than real.

Stevens constantly wrote about schemes involving foreigners. He looked for plots everywhere, and questioned the personal integrity of anyone who may have disagreed with American policy, including British Minister James Wodehouse, who had lived in Hawai'i for 20 years. Stevens' confidential letters to U.S. Secretaries of State James Blaine and John Foster raised rumors that the Queen was having a love affair with one of her staff.

Stevens' public attitude toward Queen Lili'uokalani was stiff, and often impolite. The Queen wrote:

> ...It must be said that he was either mentally incapable of recognizing what is to be expected of a gentleman, to say nothing of a diplomatist, or he was decidedly in league with those persons who had conspired against the peace of Hawai'i....[56]

Stevens viewed Hawai'i as "a semi-barbaric monarchy."[57] He described Kalākaua's regime as "an era of bombastic display of political corruption and gross immorality",[58] and accused Lili'uokalani of being a rigid monarch.[59]

In confidential diplomatic reports as the U.S. Minister to Hawai'i, Stevens wrote passionately for annexation. He believed that the United States had "a national mission to take up the 'white man's burden' – to civilize, Christianize, and extend the area of freedom to politically incompetent natives and races."[60]

- the Reform Party, supported by the descendants of the missionaries, the recently arrived Caucasian merchants and professionals, and the Caucasians who controlled the Cabinet Government

- a new party called the National Reform Party or Hui Kālai'āina, led by Robert Wilcox, and supported by native Hawaiians whose main objectives were to restore the 1864 constitutional system, to stop the continued import of Asian laborers, and to prevent annexation to the U.S.

Kalākaua's luck finally improved when native Hawaiians regained control of the Legislature through the Hui Kālai'āina Party, and voted the Reform Party out of power.

A historian and "reformer", W. D. Alexander explained it this way in a February 7, 1890 letter to his son: "One element, which turned the scales against us, was the strong anti-American feeling of the British and many of the Germans, to say nothing of the natives and half-whites."[61]

The Caucasians were not all united behind the Reform Party. On the other hand, the native Hawaiians voted against the Reform Party.

The King, who was not free to appoint the Cabinet Ministers he truly wanted, could now appoint a Cabinet that would be "less hostile" to him. King Kalākaua appointed one part-Hawaiian, one British-born, and two American-born to his new Cabinet.

Nevertheless, from defeat,

William D. Alexander

the "reformers" found a cause to unify them, aided by U.S. Minister Stevens, who encouraged Hawaiian League members to pursue annexation.

Just six months after arriving in Hawai'i, Stevens sent this confidential message to U.S. Secretary of State James Blaine, on March 20, 1890:

> To secure the influence over them (Hawai'i) which the United States has so long considered its right and duty to maintain, some decisive steps must be taken which, in the past, were not of pressing necessity.[62]

By late July, Rear Admiral George Brown, commanding the U. S. Naval Forces, Pacific Squadron, described the volatile events in a letter to Secretary of the Navy B. F. Tracy:

> In reference to political matters in the Hawaiian Islands...many events have transpired in Honolulu which indicate that serious trouble, if not a revolution, is imminent, at no distant day...The discordant element in the National Reform Party (Hui Kālai'āina), as represented by several natives and half-castes in the Legislature, who were prominent leaders in the attempted revolution of July, 1889, will not cease their revolutionary discussions and movements either in the Legislature or in public meetings on the streets. Their efforts are now being made in favor of a constitutional convention, with a review of revising the present constitution, which was adopted in 1887...

> The presence of the force under my command has a marked influence on the would-be revolutionists, as while they are aware that I am here to protect the persons and properties of citizens of the United States, the general belief among them is that I will, in the event of a revolution, take a more decided stand in the interests of those opposed to them than I might be warranted in doing. The white

residents and natives and half-castes who stand ready to
oppose the revolutionists have every confidence in their
ability to do so successfully, and take great comfort in the
knowledge of an adequate naval force being present....[63]

By opposing native Hawaiian desires for a new constitution,
and supporting the Caucasian-imposed Bayonet Constitution,
Admiral Brown is yet another prominent American official advo-
cating the interests of foreigners over native Hawaiians, who were
a majority of the electorate.

When a legislative resolution appealed to the new Ministers
to consider a new constitution, the President of the Legislature
commented in jest, that the sponsor of the resolution "might as
well ask the Ministers if they intended to hold a revolution."[64]

The remark reflected the temper of the times.

Wilcox and others continued to press for a new constitution, much like the 1864 document. He led a mass public
meeting which petitioned the King to call for a constitutional
convention.

On August 15, Kalākaua found the confidence to exert his
desires and ask the Legislature for a constitutional convention.
Without consulting his Ministers, he sent a message to the
Legislature that it was his "Royal Pleasure that the Legislative
Assembly...take such measures as would carry out the intention of
the people expressed in that petition."[65]

U.S. Minister Stevens reported to Blaine in a confidential
letter of August 19:

> The businessmen and the more responsible citizens of
> the islands are greatly disturbed. For good reasons they fear
> to have the country convulsed by such an issue. The
> English Commissioner and the undersigned have been
> urged confidentially by the leading members of the Cabinet
> and by the most conservative of the Legislature to counsel
> the King against the rash and dangerous step.

Stevens added these harsh words about King Kalākaua:

> He and a few corrupt parasites are at the center of the conspiracy (to change the constitution), back of which is a big loan in London for their corrupt handling.[66]

James Wodehouse

Ten days later, Stevens and British Minister James Wodehouse met with the King and expressed their opposition to his plans.

Wodehouse describes in a confidential report what they told the King:

> We said, whatever grievances Hawaiians might have to complain of under the present constitution, and we did not say that there were none, a means for redressing them is provided by the constitution. To go outside of that would be to get on dangerous and revolutionary ground.[67]

Both Stevens and Wodehouse asked their respective governments for naval ships to be permanently harbored in Hawai'i.

Kalākaua was so angry with the diplomats' advice, he secretly asked the British Government to replace Wodehouse with "some person more lively to the British interest."[68]

The King's appeal was ignored.

The movement for a constitutional convention led Wilcox to declare in the Legislature on September 9:

> There was danger of another revolution and the streets being made sticky with blood, if the wishes of the people were to be persistently thwarted as at present. It would be

a worse revolution than that of 1887, and some of the finest
buildings in Honolulu would be blown up.[69]

Soon after Wilcox's inflammatory speech, British Minister
Wodehouse wrote: "My colleague (Stevens) and I, have, under these
circumstances, called upon the commanders of our national ships to
hold themselves in readiness for any emergency."[70]

About the same time, the Legislature rejected a bill for a
constitutional convention.

The strain of political upheaval and loss of authority was too
much for Kalākaua to endure. Just three months later, on January
20, 1891, King Kalākaua died at age 54 of kidney disease while
visiting San Francisco to improve his health. His younger sister,
Princess Liliʻuokalani, who would become a widow eight months
later, became Queen at age 52. She immediately moved against
the "reformers" by giving Kalākaua a large funeral, and appoint-
ing a Cabinet of her choice.

Liliʻuokalani didn't want to repeat the same mistakes as her
brother. She wanted to rule, not follow. Where Kalākaua was
easy-going, she was strong-willed and uncompromising. She
lacked the shrewd political skills that might have helped her gain
support from radical Caucasians and Hawaiians. Instead, these
political groups grew more energetic and radical as they unified
against her for a more representative government.

Queen Liliʻuokalani immediately made plans for a new constitution − an act that would trigger a political crisis, and lead to
events that would bring down the Hawaiian Kingdom.

Radicals Seek Power

"(If) you come to Washington with an annexation proposition, you will find an exceedingly sympathetic administration here."
—U.S. Navy Secretary B.F. Tracy to Lorrin Thurston

"The golden hour is near at hand."
—U.S. Minister John Stevens

Sugar Problems Greet the Queen

Queen Lili'uokalani's brief reign was immediately troubled by the woes of a severe economic depression, created by a new American tax known as the McKinley Tariff.

This tariff overruled the tax-free provisions of the U.S.-Hawai'i Reciprocity Treaty by raising the tax on Hawaiian sugar imported into the United States. As a consequence, Hawai'i sugar planters lost $12 million.[1] Once again, Hawai'i suffered when a foreign nation broke a treaty negotiated in good faith. The new American tax took effect on April 1, 1891, barely three months after Lili'uokalani became Queen.

Hawaii's diplomatic representatives in Washington urged U.S. President Benjamin Harrison to abide by the Reciprocity Treaty. The President replied with a non-committal statement on October 14:

I have not yet considered the subject sufficiently to have an opinion as to how far we can go in extending our trade relations, but the necessity of maintaining and increasing our hold and influence in the Sandwich Islands is very apparent and very pressing.[2]

To overcome the inequitable economic effects of the McKinley Tariff, the Hawaiian Government had to do something drastic to satisfy American political interests. By political necessity, Hawai'i was now willing to give up Pearl Harbor.

U.S. Secretary of State James Blaine and Dr. John Mott-Smith, Hawaiian Special Envoy to the United States, negotiated such a treaty.

Hopes for the treaty, however, were short-lived.

President Harrison rejected the treaty. He preferred "high protection" of American-grown sugar over "free trade" with Hawai'i, as required by the U.S.-Hawai'i Reciprocity Treaty.[3]

The unsuccessful Blaine-Mott-Smith treaty attempt stirred debate in Hawai'i that lasted many months. On July 9, 1892, Robert Wilcox – the leader of the 1889 rebellion – introduced a resolution in the Hawai'i Legislature demanding the cession of Pearl Harbor to the U.S., and reparations to Hawai'i "for the injury inflicted by the McKinley bill."[4]

Native Hawaiians protested, so Wilcox withdrew the resolution. Wilcox continued to raise the issue whenever he wanted to criticize "the bad guidance of an unpopular Ministry."[5]

For vastly different reasons, the Pearl Harbor cession had become a political bargaining chip for both annexationists and increasingly vocal native Hawaiian opponents of the Queen. The annexationists wanted Hawai'i to be fully American, while politically radical native Hawaiians anticipated economic benefits that would result from American development of Pearl Harbor.

Wilcox explained: "If America gains possession of Pearl Harbor, she will spend millions of money there."[6]

The meager Kingdom treasury constantly needed money. Hawaii's major revenue source, the property tax, provided insufficient funds, especially since the major plantation landowners were subsidized with low property taxes on agricultural land.

Furthermore, the Caucasian "reformers" objected to alternative arrangements that Lili'uokalani and her predecessor, Kalākaua, made to keep the Kingdom afloat – especially the controversial revenue-raising lottery and opium-licensing bills.

Native Hawaiians are Divided

Queen Liliʻuokalani

By 1891 and 1892, Queen Liliʻuokalani's policies had the unintended consequence of increasing annexation sentiment.

After the defeat of the Reform Party in the 1890 elections, radical Caucasians convinced conservative Reform Party members to alter their agenda. They no longer pursued a more stable government or a constitutional monarchy. Annexation was now their goal.

As a sign of increasing political activity, the number of political parties campaigning during the 1892 elections doubled from two to four. The three major political parties were: the Reform Party, the National Reform Party, and a new Liberal Party (which included Robert Wilcox and many former followers of the National Reform Party).

Both the new Liberal Party and the National Reform Party were supported primarily by native Hawaiians. The more radical Liberal Party desired not to preserve the monarchy but to establish a representative form of government. The Liberal Party opposed the Cabinet, the Queen, and her advisors. This created internal dissension among native Hawaiians, and divided their numerical voting strength.

The Liberal Party called attention to the "rotten condition of officialdom" in the Kingdom. Robert Wilcox criticized the:

...utter misgovernment of affairs at home. Ignorant fools are conducting the Government...and (influencing) the Queen...It is a standing disgrace to the Hawaiian nation...We must all be loyal Hawaiians, and tell the Queen that her present Government is an injustice and a disgrace to the nation. We must not flatter her.

Wilcox added, "To flatter the Queen would be to inflate her with her own importance, which would cause disastrous results."[7]

Who could the Queen turn to for trusted political advice? The 1887 Bayonet Constitution removed the monarch's strong powers of days gone by, forcing her to yield to the wishes of the Caucasians, who controlled the House of Nobles and the Cabinet. On the other hand, the success of the native Hawaiian-supported Liberal Party owed its credibility to that quagmire.

In the scramble for votes in the 1892 election, no political party captured a majority of seats. This left the Legislature divided and weak for most of the year.

John E. Bush, a Liberal Party leader, said:

The practical defeat of the Liberal Party is the lost opportunity of the Hawaiians...It looks now as though the only hope for equal rights in this country lies in – shall we say it – annexation.[8]

U.S. Minister Stevens Plots Annexation

U.S. Secretary of State James Blaine continued to pursue a manifest destiny policy for the United States. He sent this blunt communication to President Harrison on August 10:

...I think there are only three places that are of value enough to be taken, that are not continental. One is Hawai'i and the others are Cuba and Porto Rico (sic). Cuba and Porto Rico (sic) are not now imminent and will not be for a generation. Hawai'i may come up for decision at any

unexpected hour and I hope we shall be prepared to decide
it in the affirmative....[9]

During Stevens' three and-a-half year diplomatic assignment
in Hawai'i, he encouraged annexation with American residents.
Friends and foes of annexation said Stevens met often with
annexationists such as Thurston, who admitted in his memoirs
that Stevens showed him diplomatic messages. Thurston probably shared with Stevens the plans of the Annexation Club.

It is easy to be awed by the bluntness of Stevens' words, most
of which were penned under the stamp of "confidential".

For example, Stevens tried to justify annexation through
imperialism in a September 5, 1891 letter to Blaine:

> Great Britain, France, Germany and Spain have taken
> possession of nearly all of the principal groups in the South
> Pacific and of the small isolated islands in the Central
> Pacific. If the Hawaiian group should slip from our control,
> our national rivals would gain great naval and commercial
> advantage in the North Pacific, whose dominance fairly
> belongs to the United States. Nothing can be plainer than
> that it is our imperative duty to hold these islands with the
> firm resolution and the invincible strength of the American
> nation. To ignore their prospective value...would be one of
> those blunders which justly have their place among the
> crimes of statesmen.
>
> ...Inevitably (these islands) must continue under the
> increased fostering care of the United States, or fall under
> foreign control.

Stevens added that the "present Reciprocity Treaty (has)...much
increased American interests and influence here" but America's
repeal of the sugar tax exemption by the McKinley Tariff, sponsored by America's future President, has dealt Hawai'i "a very
severe blow" and threatens bankruptcy as "the inevitable fate" of

many sugar planters and businesses. [10]

A month later, Stevens informed Blaine: "...Now is a
good time to secure Pearl Harbor in practical perpetuity."[11]

Stevens felt confident the
Reform Party would win the
upcoming 1892 elections. In
two letters dated February 8,
1892, as well as in many others, Stevens referred to Americans, businessmen and Caucasians as responsible parties, and
to the native Hawaiians and
Asians as irresponsible.
Stevens wrote boldly of annexation desires. After the Reci-

Princess Kaʻiulani

procity Treaty is ratified, Stevens urged a "new departure" of
American policy is "rapidly becoming a necessity."

He added:

> ...Annexation must be the future remedy or else Great
> Britain will be furnished with circumstances and opportu-
> nity to get a hold of these islands....

Stevens also revealed:

> The intelligent and responsible men here, unaided by
> outside support, are too few in numbers to control political
> affairs and to serve good government.[12]

After the Reform Party lost the 1892 elections, an obviously
frustrated Stevens looked for conspiracies everywhere. He informed Secretary of State Blaine that the half-British heir-appar-

ent Princess Ka'iulani and other native Hawaiians would overthrow the Queen, establish a Republic, and seek annexation:

> ...I have information which I deem reliable that there is
> an organized revolutionary party on the islands, composed
> largely of native Hawaiians and a considerable number of
> whites and half whites, led chiefly by individuals of the
> latter two classes.

Other militant native Hawaiians, Stevens wrote, are "opposed to the Queen," and are "especially opposed to the half-
English heir apparent, now being educated in England." Stevens
added that these Hawaiians may "overthrow the monarchy and
establish a Republic with the ultimate view of annexation to the
United States of the whole islands...."
Stevens asked Blaine for instructions if a native Hawaiian
uprising overthrows the monarchy by peaceful means:

> ...Would the United States Minister and Naval Com-
> mander here be justified in responding affirmatively to the
> call of the members of the removed Government to restore
> them to power or replace in the possession of the Govern-
> ment buildings?

> Or should the United States Minister and Naval Com-
> mander confine themselves exclusively to the preservation
> of American property, the protection of American citizens,
> and the prevention of anarchy?

> ...In such contingencies, would it be justifiable to use
> the United States forces here to restore the Government
> buildings to the possession of the displaced officials?

> ...I desire to know how far the present Minister and
> Naval Commander may deviate from established interna-
> tional rules and precedents....[13]

Later that month, nearly a year before the overthrow of the Hawaiian monarchy, Stevens reported to Blaine:

> The time is not distant when the United States must say yes or no to the question of 'annexation' – that the moral and pecuniary welfare of these islands will demand an affirmative answer.[14]

Stevens revealed details of his plan to Blaine in a confidential letter dated April 2. Stevens said that property holders (i.e., Americans) would support annexation "...provided...(they) could get any encouragement that the United States would take these islands as a territory."

In that same letter, Stevens expressed an intense hostility toward the monarchy: "For 20 years the Palace has been the center of corruption and scandal, and is likely to remain as long as the Hawaiian native monarchy exists."[15]

Other American officials felt strongly about annexing Hawai'i. Rear Admiral George Brown, Commander of the U.S. Naval Force, Pacific Station, notified the U.S. Secretary of the Navy that the Queen might abdicate if she received a good financial settlement.[16]

James Blaine resigned as Secretary of State in late June, supposedly to run for President again, and was replaced by John Foster. In correspondence to Foster, Stevens stepped-up his criticism of the Hawaiian monarchy, and issued a plea for action.

On November 20 Stevens sent U.S. Secretary of State Foster a confidential and detailed summary of "explosive conditions in the Islands." He expressed concerns of a possible Hawaiian alignment with England, and wrote unfavorably of both Queen Lili'uokalani and Princess Ka'iulani:

> ...The present sovereign is not expected to live many years. The princess heir apparent has always been, and is likely always to be, under English influence. Her father is

British in blood and prejudices, firmly entrenched here as collector customs, an important and influential office. She has been for some years and still is in England; her patron there who has a kind of guardianship of her, T. H. Davies, is a Troy Englishman, who lived here many years, who still owns large property in the islands, and is a resolute and persistent opponent of American acquisition of Pearl Harbor. Mr. Wodehouse, the English Minister, has long resided here; his eldest son is married to a half-caste sister of the Crown Princess...The death of the present Queen, therefore, would virtually place an English princess on the Hawaiian throne, and put in the hands of the ultra-English the patronage and influence of the palace...

Now for his pro-annexation opinions:

...Destiny and the vast future interest of the United States in the Pacific clearly indicate who at no distant day must be responsible for the government of the islands. Under a territorial government they could be as easily governed as any of the existing territories of the United States...I can not now refrain from expressing the opinion with emphasis that the golden hour is near at hand...

Stevens charged:

One of two courses seems to me absolutely necessary to be followed: Either bold and vigorous measures for annexation or...Pearl Harbor perpetually ceded to the United States with an implied but not necessarily American protectorate over the islands.

...Which of the two lines of policy and action shall be adopted our statesmen and our government must decide. Certain it is that the interests of the United States and the welfare of these islands will not permit the continuance of the existing state and tendency of things. Having for so many years extended a helping hand to the islands and encouraging the American residents and their friends at home to the extent we have, we can not refrain now from aiding them with vigorous measures, without injury to ourselves and those of our 'kith and kin,' and without neglecting American opportunities that never seemed so obvious and pressing as they do now...

Stevens concluded with an unmistakable call for annexation:

The strong inclination of several European powers to gain possession of all the islands in the Pacific, except (those) protected by the United States, is plainly shown by what has taken place in recent years.

The value of the Hawaiian Islands to the United States for commercial and naval purposes has been well understood by American statesmen for more than half a century.

To postpone American action many years is only to add to present unfavorable tendencies and to make future possession more difficult.

Americanize the islands, assume control of the 'crown lands.'

Stevens recommended buying Hawai'i for $100,000.[17]

Stevens' illustrative phrase, "the golden hour is near at hand," reveals much about both Stevens' and America's role and participation in the fall of the Hawaiian Kingdom, and subsequent annexation.

This important letter strengthens the evidence that dethronement and annexation were considered and encouraged by the United States several years before the 1898 Spanish-American War, which is often mistakenly cited as the sole reason for annexing the Islands.

Otherwise it would seem unusual that a U.S. diplomat would consider such a revolutionary and violent course against the peaceful Hawaiian Kingdom, allied to the United States by friendship treaties.

In the same letter, Stevens specifically referred to Schofield and Alexander's secret 1873 military survey of Pearl Harbor. The State Department and military must have shared a great deal of information about Hawai'i! Stevens' knowledge of the secret 1873 military mapping expedition can not be ignored.

Annexation Club Established

The pace of events which culminated in overthrow and annexation, were heating-up. Between the February, 1892 election and the opening of the Legislature in May, two major developments occurred, giving new opportunities to the radical Caucasian political opponents of the Queen.

- Liberal Party leaders stepped-up their instigation of anti-government agitation, and

- Caucasians established the Annexation Club.

Sensitive to criticism, the Ministers who ran the Government reacted to the Liberal Party conspiracy and possible revolutionary actions by arresting many Liberal Party leaders.

According to Thurston's memoirs, the Annexation Club was established in either January or February 1892:

> ...not to promote annexation, but to be ready to act quickly and intelligently, should Lili'uokalani precipitate the necessity by some move against the constitution, tending to revert to absolutism or anything of the nature.[18]

The Annexation Club had no more than 17 members – 13 of

Annexation Club

whom, a year later, were named to a Committee of Safety that dethroned the monarchy with the assistance of U.S. Minister Stevens and American troops.

Thurston said Club members ought to "know beforehand the probable attitude of the United States Government toward annexing Hawai'i," so the organization sent him to Washington in March, 1892 to learn what he could. [19]

While in Washington, Thurston met briefly with House Foreign Relations Committee chairman James Blount, and held encouraging meetings with U.S. Secretary of State Blaine and Secretary of the Navy Tracy.

After Thurston gave Blaine a letter of introduction from U.S. Minister John Stevens, Blaine spoke openly about prospects for American annexation. Thurston then gave Blaine a detailed explanation of political and economic affairs in Hawai'i, and said it was difficult to maintain peace because:

> ...Lili'uokalani was likely at any time to attempt the promulgation of a new constitution. If she tended toward

absolutism, we proposed to seek annexation to the United States, provided it would entertain the proposal. A nucleus had been formed in Honolulu to bring the plan to a focus, should occasion arise; that nucleus had sent me to Washington to ascertain the attitude of the authorities there. [20]

Blaine told Thurston he considered "the subject of the utmost importance," and advised him to see Secretary of the Navy B. F. Tracy, and to "tell him what you have told me, and say to him that I think you should see the President." Then, "come to me after you have seen President Harrison." Thurston called upon Secretary Tracy, and the two men walked to the White House, where Thurston waited a half-hour while Tracy spoke with President Harrison. Tracy told Thurston:

...The President...authorizes me to say to you that, if conditions in Hawai'i compel you people to act as you have indicated, and you come to Washington with an annexation proposition, you will find an exceedingly sympathetic administration here.

Thurston wrote, "That was all I wanted to know."[21]

Encouraged by his visit, Thurston wrote Blaine a long letter on May 27 about "threatening revolution and disturbance."

Thurston identified specific island conditions which he felt would culminate in annexation to the United States or England. He described a plan that the Annexation Club would pursue and recommended offering the Queen a generous pension to encourage her to retire. Otherwise "it will be necessary to use such force in removing her as is necessary, and the establishing of a Provisional Government until union with the United States is completed."

Thurston preferred: "securing the appointment of a Cabinet in the Islands committed to annexation" and educating the people to support annexation. Then, if the U.S. Congress agreed, he would encourage the Hawaiian Legislature to vote for annexation.[22]

Thurston wrote:

> ...Every interest, political, commercial, financial and
> previous friendship points in the direction of the United
> States; but they feel that if they cannot secure the desired
> union with the United States, a union with England would
> be preferable to a continuance under existing circum-
> stances....[23]

Thurston argued that annexation was favored due to the
"changed conditions brought about by the McKinley Tariff bill."
The tariff act had driven the price of sugar down from $100 to $60
a ton, forcing planters to sell their sugar "at less than the cost of
production...."[24]

Thurston described a racially divided Kingdom with "an
overwhelming majority in one class (the natives), and the ownership of practically all the property in another class (the foreigners)."

He reported to Blaine that only 4,000 of the 15,000 voters
are foreigners. Thurston admitted, people are "split" into "factions, along color and race lines...."[25]

Thurston's letter to Blaine reveal that someone, probably
Stevens, had been keeping the United States Government well-
informed about the growing annexation movements in Hawai'i.

Stevens fueled the annexationists, encouraged the Liberal
Party members, and enraged royalists, when, during a July 4th
celebration speech, he arrogantly called Hawai'i a "monarch
cursed country," a phrase reported in a prominent American
publication, *The Nation.*[26]

Intrigue and rumors filled Hawaii's coconut pipeline. On
October 12, 1892, Captain Gilbert Wiltse of the *U.S.S. Boston,*
anchored in Honolulu harbor, wrote to the Secretary of the Navy:

> There is a large and growing sentiment, particularly
> among the planters, in favor of annexation to the United

States, but I am informed that the leaders do nothing until an opportune moment will arrive for some time to come. However, everything seems to point toward an eventual request for annexation.[27]

Stevens sent to Foster a 44-page report supporting annexation on November 20:

> The monarchy is now only an impediment to good government – an obstruction to the prosperity and progress of the islands...Hawai'i has reached the parting of the ways. She must now take the road which leads to Asia, or the other, which outlets her in America, gives her an American civilization and binds her to the care of American destiny.[28]

Archibald Hopkins, the Annexation Club representative in Washington, D.C., sent Thurston a surprising letter dated November 15. Hopkins wrote:

> I am authorized to inform you that the United States Government will pay to Queen Lili'uokalani and those connected with her, the sum of $250,000, for the assignment to the United States of the Sovereignty of Hawai'i. [29]

Thurston, who was returning to Hawai'i from Chicago, thought the price was extravagant. Thurston replied to Hopkins:

> The United States Minister at Honolulu, Mr. Stevens, has written and forwarded by this mail, an exhaustive dispatch to the State Department concerning the Hawaiian situation. He allowed me to read it, and I heartily endorse every statement in it. [30]

How much did Thurston and Stevens know about each other's plans and activities...and when did they know it?

In a letter to Archibald Hopkins, the Annexation Club's agent in Washington, Thurston credited Stevens with having "the fullest knowledge of the facts," and for being "an enthusiastic advocate of annexation."[31]

About the same time, Secretary of Navy Tracy told Admiral Joseph Skerrett, who was preparing to embark on a return assignment to Hawai'i: "Commodore, the wishes of the Government have changed (in the last 20 years). They will be very glad to annex Hawai'i...(through) legal means...."[32]

Native Hawaiians Seek a New Constitution

No single political party won the 1892 election with a clear majority of legislative seats. This resulted in an eight month struggle to secure a stable Cabinet. As a result, four different Cabinets were appointed and removed, depending on whatever political coalitions were forged among the three major political parties.

Little was accomplished during the turmoil of the longest-ever, 171-day Legislature. By the year's end, the Legislature finally considered three controversial bills: to establish a lottery, to regulate and license opium sales, and to call for a constitutional convention.

Vigorous opposition of the Queen's Cabinet could not deter the Legislature from passing the lottery and opium bills. The Queen signed both bills into law. The new laws would inject a permanent source of up to several hundred thousand dollars of annual revenue for the Kingdom, and would relieve the Government from continually borrowing money. The Queen and a majority of legislators felt it was better to regulate and tax the underground opium business than to allow illegal smuggling to continue unchecked.

Finance Minister William Cornwell, an opponent of the lottery bill, admitted that it was "... supported by nearly all the Americans in Honolulu, the very men who revolted and now claim the lottery was the cause of the revolution."[33]

Regarding the constitution, it was no secret that Lili'uokalani, as had Kalākaua, felt severely limited by the restrictions placed on the monarchy by the Bayonet Constitution. Now, feeling that she had the will of the people who backed the Liberal Party's call for a new constitution, Lili'uokalani felt confident to exert leadership. She was ready to give a majority of the voters what they wanted – a new constitution.

During the 1892 election campaigns, Lili'uokalani acknowledged, "Petitions poured in from every part of the Islands for a new constitution" signed by about two-thirds of the registered voters (6,500 of 9,000 electors). "To have ignored or disregarded so general a request," the Queen said she would have to be "deaf to the voice of the people...."[34]

Buoyed by the strength of the Liberal Party in the 1892 election, and the native support for a new constitution, Queen Lili'uokalani quietly drafted a new constitution in October 1892.

This new constitution would free the monarchy from the shackles of the Bayonet Constitution. It would give the monarchy greater power, give the vote to Hawaiian-born or naturalized citizens, remove certain property qualifications that prevented native Hawaiians from voting for the House of Nobles, and would make Cabinet Ministers subject to removal by the Legislature.

The Queen told her Cabinet Ministers about the draft constitution. At least two of her four Ministers promised their support prior to their appointment. The Queen asked Attorney General Arthur Peterson to review the draft constitution and to make recommendations, but he never did. He told the Queen he never read her document.

Queen Lili'uokalani decided to proclaim the new constitution immediately after the Legislature adjourned. Every constitution – 1840, 1852, 1864, and even 1877 – was granted by the ruling monarch, not the Legislature.

In her autobiography, Queen Lili'uokalani wrote emphatically about the monarch's power:

Let it be repeated: the promulgation of a new constitution, adapted to the needs of the times and the demands of the people, had been an indisputable prerogative of the Hawaiian monarchy.[35]

Representative G. Kamauoha summed-up how native Hawaiian legislators felt about the Queen's Cabinet:

The Cabinet were honest and able men. There was no doubt that they possessed the confidence of the community. They were men of integrity...but would they carry out the wishes of the Queen? Would they do what the Queen and the Hawaiian people wanted in regard to the lottery, the constitutional convention, etc.? Would they do as the Queen wanted them to do? [36]

Probably not.

Queen Lili'uokalani Yields to an American Conspiracy

"I think you have a great opportunity."
—U.S. Minister John Stevens

U.S. Warship Takes Gun Practice

On January 4, 1893, the *U.S.S. Boston* steamed out of Honolulu Harbor for 10 days of "a long-needed target practice" near Hilo.[1]

U.S. Minister John Stevens sailed with the warship during the mission, allegedly for a vacation.

The gunnery practice may have been a carefully planned maneuver intended to prepare U.S. marines and the ship's cannons for combat. Or perhaps the target practice was intended to impress Japan, which Stevens feared would act to protect its 30,000 sugar plantation contract laborers in Hawai'i.

Stevens admitted under oath, that he and Captain Wiltse discussed plans for landing troops during their 10-day voyage.[2] Perhaps Stevens had already promised the annexation-minded Americans that he would support them with American troops.

For months, rumors in Honolulu suggested that the Queen would proclaim a new constitution, but no one knew when. Would Queen Lili'uokalani dare to publicly challenge the political power of the Caucasians?

Saturday, January 14
The Queen Seeks a New Constitution

About 10:00 a.m., the Queen announced to her Ministers that she would proclaim a new constitution that afternoon.

Arthur Peterson

John Colburn

The Ministers argued with the Queen about the propriety of proclaiming a new constitution. When Attorney General Peterson said he hadn't read the document, the Queen got angry.

"You had it for a month," Lili'uokalani charged. "Why haven't you read it?"

Peterson didn't reply.

The Queen's desire for a new constitution was supported by the native Hawaiian people, but her Cabinet advisors embarrassed her. They backed down. They feared a new constitution would stir trouble in the Caucasian community. They were right.

After the hasty Cabinet meeting, two Ministers, John F. Colburn, Minister of the Interior, and Attorney General Arthur Peterson ran to see Lorrin Thurston, William Smith and former Judge Alfred Hartwell, to report the Queen's intentions. The three annexationists advised Colburn and Peterson to oppose the Queen's efforts. Smith described Colburn as "a scared man – frightened."[3]

When the Legislature adjourned at noon, a confident Queen Lili'uokalani stood poised and ready to declare a new constitution. It was her prerogative, as monarch. She explained in her autobiography:

> ...I proposed to make certain changes in the Constitution of the Hawai'i Kingdom...for the advantage and benefit of the Kingdom, and subjects and residents...These proposed changes did not deprive foreigners of any rights or privileges enjoyed by them under the Constitution of 1887....[4]

Little did the Queen suspect the events which followed would culminate in the fall of the Hawaiian Kingdom.

When the *U.S.S. Boston* returned to Honolulu just before noon, Stevens stepped off the plank and into a frenzy of revolutionary activities.

Two of the Queen's Ministers, Colburn and Cornwell both said that Stevens got excited when learning that the Queen had signed the lottery bill. The 73-year old Stevens stomped his cane on the floor, slammed his fist on the table, and exclaimed: "This is a direct attack on the U.S. Government."[5]

Meanwhile, foreign diplomats, legislators, and other dignitaries sat waiting for a ceremony to begin at 'Iolani Palace. They waited for two hours, while the Queen's Cabinet found excuses not to support her constitution. When it was time for her Cabinet to step forward, sign their names and support the document, they refused. Again, they left the Palace to notify Lorrin Thurston of the Annexation Club.

The Queen wrote bitterly of her Ministers: "They had led me out to the edge of a precipice, and now were leaving me to take the step alone. It was humiliating."[6]

Reluctantly, the embarrassed and shaken Queen decided to wait until she could gain more official support. No chance. News spread fast.

Saturday burst into a busy day of public rallies and secret plots. People assembled for action, in groups large and small, for and against the Queen.

Some 1,500 to 2,000 supporters of the Liberal and National Reform Parties rallied to adopt resolutions supporting the Queen's decision not to seek another constitution, for the time being.

The radical annexationists seized the opportunity to act. By 1:30 p.m., eager annexationists Smith, Thurston, Wundenburg and Macfarlane were meeting in the Attorney General's Office with all four of the Queen's jittery Ministers – Cornwell, Colburn, Parker and Peterson.[7]

Thurston and the insurgents agreed that the throne would be declared vacant by the Queen's treasonable attitude, but the Ministers objected. Thurston drafted a declaration anyway.[8]

The meeting ended about 2:30 p.m. soon after the Queen's messenger ordered the Cabinet members to return to 'Iolani Palace.

Thirteen ambitious Caucasian businessmen eager to overthrow the monarchy, gathered at William Smith's downtown law office from mid-afternoon until dark, where they established a Committee of Public Safety.

These businessmen were experienced in revolutionary affairs. They were mostly the same men who had imposed the Bayonet Constitution on King Kalākaua, and now they were ready to push Queen Lili'uokalani off her royal throne. They did not fear the Hawaiian monarch, especially with the apparent promise of American troop support from U.S. Minister John Stevens.

These "reformers" felt compelled and perhaps overjoyed with the opportunity to depose the monarchy. Despite the powers they gained with the Bayonet Constitution, they realized that they couldn't effectively control the Cabinet government or the Legislature as long as the native Hawaiians were a majority of the voters.

All members of this Committee of Safety (except George Wilcox, a former Prime Minister) were also members of the Annexation Club.

The 13-member Committee of Safety was dominated by nine men who were Americans or had ties to the United States:

Americans: H. E. Cooper, F. W. McChesney, T. F. Lansing and M. A. McCandless

Hawai'i-born of American parents: W. O. Smith, Lorrin Thurston, W. R. Castle and A. S. Wilcox

Naturalized Hawaiian citizens: W. C. Wilder (American), and C. Bolte (German), and Henry Waterhouse (Tasmanian)

German: H. F. Glade

Scotch: Andrew Brown

Two members, Glade and Wilcox resigned one to two days later, and were replaced by Ed Suhr (German) and John Emmeluth (American).[9]

As the Committee's first order of business, Lorrin Thurston, the most visible agitator, proposed "annexation to the United States."[10]

The Committee approved the resolution by a 12-1 vote. George Wilcox, the lone dissenter, resigned and returned home to Kaua'i.

A special subcommittee, led by Thurston, immediately visited Minister Stevens to seek his support. According to Smith, U.S. Minister Stevens told Thurston:

> ...The United States troops on board the *U.S.S. Boston* would be ready to land any moment to prevent the destruction of American life and property, and in regard to the matter of establishing a Provisional Government they of course recognize the existing government whatever it might be.[11]

According to Thurston, Stevens told the Queen:

...He (Stevens) considered the position taken by the
Cabinet and people a just and legal one, and the attempt
made by the Queen a revolutionary one; and that if asked
by her for his support he would not give it; and...he should
recognize the Cabinet as the supporters of law and as
possessing the authority of government so long as they
were supported by any respectable number of responsible
citizens.... [12]

When Thurston asked Stevens what requirements were necessary for being considered the "existing government", Stevens
gave a specific reply. He would recognize:

Whatever government was established and was actually in possession of the Government Building, the executive departments and Archives, and in possession of the
city, that was a de facto government proclaiming itself a
government....[13]

Stevens told the Committee of Safety exactly which buildings
they should occupy, and encouraged them to proceed with their
plans. Then Stevens sent a man to rent a building to house
American troops from the *U.S.S. Boston*. The Committee fully
expected American military and diplomatic support. After all,
their intent was not just a revolution, but the fulfillment of a
dream, annexation.

Stevens' annexation views were well known in Hawai'i, and
his close association with the Caucasians made it clear that he
favored a change in government.

Stevens promised the annexationists that he would recognize
any government that the Committee might establish. The American Minister's approval, tacit or otherwise, bolstered the Committee of Safety and stiffened their resolve to overthrow the monarchy. By the evening of January 14, the Committee of Safety was
busily recruiting and arming a small revolutionary force. Plans
were well under way to topple the Hawaiian monarchy.

Samuel Damon   **William O. Smith**

That evening, Committee members met again. They invited a leading conservative, Sanford Dole, Associate Justice of the Hawaiian Supreme Court, to join them. Dole said he wasn't prepared to overthrow the Queen, but he would help draft documents for a Provisional Government.

Sunday, January 15
A Day for Making Plans

Insurgent F. Wundenburg recalled this day was as quiet as a Sunday. "I do not think anyone knew what was going on except the politicians and those who were behind the scenes, as you might say."[14]

Before dawn, at 6:00 a.m., Thurston met with two members of the Queen's Cabinet, Colburn and Peterson. He told them about the Committee's meeting with Stevens the prior evening, and that the Committee would not let matters rest, even if the Queen promised not to proclaim a new constitution. The Committee, he said, intended to declare the throne vacant. In an attempt to head off further trouble, the Queen's Cabinet prepared a formal statement that the Queen would not seek another constitution.

The Committee of Safety continued to meet and make plans throughout the day and into the evening.

That evening, Cabinet members Parker and Peterson called upon Minister Stevens to learn what Stevens would do if there was an armed insurrection. The Cabinet members left the meeting deeply troubled that Stevens would not publicly support the present Kingdom Government. The Ministers agreed that the government should not take any direct action against the Committee.

Stevens told different stories to the royalists and insurgents. He told the Queen's Ministers he was a neutral diplomat, while he assured the Committee of his support.

This day was spent talking and planning.

Monday, January 16
American Troops Sent Ashore

This day, the Queen's Ministers posted notices announcing that the Queen would not promulgate a new constitution.

Thurston and Smith again visited Minister Stevens. They told Stevens about the Committee's plans, and asked for his support, in case they should be arrested. Stevens knew, in advance, that the Committee was going to try to overthrow the monarchy. Attorney William Smith said that Stevens "gave assurances of his earnest purpose to afford all the protection that was in his power to protect life and property."[15]

F. Wundenberg, a leading insurgent who commanded the station house for the Provisional Government, candidly admitted that the insurgents were weak and disorganized, and that Stevens promised to protect them with American soldiers:

During all the deliberations of the Committee (of Safety), and in fact, throughout the whole proceedings connected with plans for the move up to the final issue, the basis of action was the general understanding that Minister Stevens would keep his promise to support the movement with the men from the *Boston,* and the statement is advisedly made – with a full knowledge of the lack of arms, ammunition, and men; also the utter absence of organization at all adequate to the undertaking – that without the previous assurance of the support from the American Minister, and the actual presence of the United States troops, no movement would have been attempted, and, if attempted, would have been a dismal failure, resulting in the capture or death of the participants in a very short time.[16]

Other Committee members, including Samuel Damon later testified that Stevens assured the Committee of Safety that they would receive support from American soldiers. Two Cabinet members, Colburn and Parker, confirmed in conversations with Smith and Thurston, that Stevens said he would call out the troops.[17]

The Committee of Safety handed Stevens this letter, asking for protection, and for the landing of American troops:

Hawaiian Islands,
Honolulu, January 16, 1893

We, the undersigned, citizens and residents of Honolulu, respectfully represent that, in view of recent public events in this Kingdom, culminating in the revolutionary acts of Queen Liliʻuokalani on Saturday last, the public safety is menaced and lives and property are in peril, and we appeal to you and the United States forces at your command for assistance.

The Queen, with the aid of armed force and accompanied by threats of violence and bloodshed from those with

whom she was acting, attempted to proclaim a new constitution; and while prevented for the time from accomplish-
ing her object, declared publicly that she would only defer
her action.

This conduct and action was upon an occasion and
under circumstance(s) which have created general alarm
and terror.

We are unable to protect ourselves without aid and,
therefore, pray for the protection of the United States
forces.

Committee of Safety[18]

The Committee's request was written in general terms which
failed to specifically ask for protection of American lives and
property. More importantly, the Committee expressed an inabil-
ity to protect itself – which Stevens deliberately failed to report
in his later messages to Washington.

That afternoon, two public meetings were held – one called
by the Queen's supporters, the other by the Committee of Safety.

Emotions were running high.

As many as 1,000 royalists attended a rally for the Queen
at the 'Iolani Palace Square. There was no reason for people
to get excited, since they could not have known about the
planned insurgency.

A few blocks away, more than 1,200 people crowded into the
Committee of Safety's well-planned afternoon rally at the Honolulu Rifles' Armory. Most of Honolulu's Caucasian male population were there, as were many curious part-Hawaiians.

Thurston fired-up the meeting with a Patrick Henry-style
"liberty or death" plea, urging the crowd to do more than just
condemn the Queen's proposal of a new constitution. He charged:

...She wants us to sleep on a slumbering volcano which
will one morning spew out blood and destroy us all...The

man who has not the spirit to rise after the menaces to our liberties has not the right to keep them. Has the tropic sun cooled and thinned our blood, or have we flowing in our veins the warm, rich blood which loves liberty and dies for it?[19]

By 4:00 p.m., after its successful mass meeting, the Committee decided to postpone further action until the next day. They believed it would benefit their objectives if they were established and officially recognized before any American troops were landed. Two Committee members visited Stevens and asked that the U.S. military landing party be detained until the next day, Tuesday.

They were too late. Stevens announced that arrangements had already been made to land the marines that very afternoon. Plans would not be altered.

According to Committee member F. Wundenberg, Stevens told them: "Gentlemen, the troops of the *Boston* land this afternoon at 5 o'clock, whether you are ready or not."[20]

Indeed, Stevens had already acted. Two hours earlier, around 3:00 p.m., Minister Stevens had boarded the *U.S.S. Boston,* and officially asked Commander Wiltse to order his troops ashore "as a precautionary measure to protect American life and property." Stevens official request read:

United States Legation
Honolulu, January 16, 1893

Sir: In view of existing critical circumstances in Honolulu, indicating an inadequate legal force, I request you to land Marines and Sailors from the ship under your command for the protection of the United States Legation, and the United States Consulate and to secure the safety of American life and property.

Very truly yours,
John L. Stevens[21]

U.S. Navy Lt. Lucien Young commanding a squad of
***U.S.S. Boston* Marines on January 17, 1893**

U.S. Navy Lt. Lucien Young wrote that Stevens told *U.S.S. Boston* Commander Wiltse: "You need not apprehend any one firing upon you, as they have never done such a thing under other and similar circumstances." Stevens was referring to the American troop landings in 1874 and 1889.

Young added: "Wiltse then read a short letter of instructions...(that) were taken bodily from his confidential letter from the Navy Department" prepared that morning.[22]

Technically, the marines couldn't land without direct orders from Stevens. Yet, at 10:00 a.m., five hours before Stevens officially requested the troops to go ashore, Captain Wiltse began making preparations for the troop landing. U.S. Navy Lt. Lucien Young wrote: "Wiltse called me to the cabin and told me that he had to land troops."[23]

Was Wiltse acting on his own, or was he getting everything ready for Stevens' formal message?

By the time Stevens boarded the *U.S.S. Boston* that afternoon,

The Government Building – Ali'iolani Hale (c) and Opera House (r). Arion Hall stood behind the Opera House – now the Post Office site, where U.S. Marines from the *U.S.S. Boston* camped.

the soldiers were fully armed and ready to go. Wiltse's written order, which complied with standard Navy policy, had been issued to Lt. Commander Swinburne, who would lead the U.S. military force:

> ...You will take command of the Battalion and land in Honolulu for the purpose of protecting our Legation, Consulate, and the lives and property of American citizens, and to assist in preserving public order. Great prudence must be exercised by both officers and men, and no action taken that is not fully warranted by the condition of affairs, and by the conduct of those who may be inimical to the treaty rights of American citizens....[24]

Just a few blocks from 'Iolani Palace, the *U.S.S. Boston* sat anchored in Honolulu Harbor – a battle cruiser with 8" and 26" high powered cannons (with 174 explosive shells) capable of leveling 'Iolani Palace and other important government buildings.

Between 4:00 to 5:00 that afternoon, as many as 162 armed U.S. Marines landed in Honolulu, carrying 14,000 rounds of rifle ammunition and 1,200 revolver cartridges. They marched down King Street, past 'Iolani Palace and halted two blocks away at King and Alapa'i Streets.

From there, some proceeded to the American Consulate at Fort and Merchant Streets, some marched to the U.S. Legation on Nu'uanu Street, while most halted at Arion Hall adjacent to the principal buildings of government.

Captain Gilbert Wiltse of the *U.S.S. Boston* leaving Hawai'i

By the next day, Tuesday, all the soldiers were camping on the grounds of Arion Hall, which Stevens had rented.

Why Arion Hall?

This strategically located downtown building stood just 30 yards from the Government Building, and a mere 200 yards from 'Iolani Palace. Arion Hall was Stevens' second choice as a military camp site.

Stevens first tried to rent the Opera House, which commanded a closer and better view of 'Iolani Palace, but the owner rejected Stevens' offer. The Opera House had been damaged by gunfire during the 1889 Wilcox Revolt. Stevens then rented Arion Hall, which was a good distance from most American property.

The Opera House and Arion Hall both stood where the downtown Post Office now stands.

U.S. Admiral Joseph Skerrett, Commander in Chief of the Pacific Station, who eventually replaced Captain Wiltse in Hawai'i, criticized the stationing of U.S. troops at Arion Hall:

Map of Downtown Honolulu
Showing 'Iolani Palace and Arion Hall

January 17, 1893

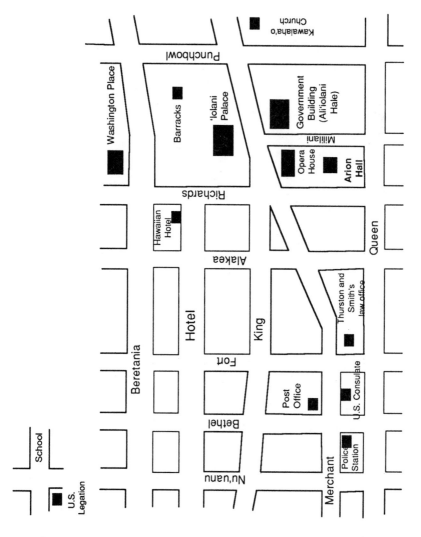

Source: map prepared by staff of W.D. Alexander, Surveyer General of Hawai'i,
for the 1894 Morgan Report (this map has been re-drawn by computer)

...it was inadvisable to locate the U.S. troops where they were quartered if they were landed for the protection of U.S. citizens and their property. If troops were landed for the protection or support of the Provisional Government, it was a wise choice....[25]

William Cornwell, a Minister in the Queen's last Cabinet, agreed:

...If the troops were landed solely for the protection of American property, the placing of them so far away from the center of the property of Americans and so very close to the property of the Hawaiian Government was remarkable and suggestive.[26]

The mere presence of American forces intimidated the Hawaiian Government, and provided psychological support for the insurgents.

The Queen and her Cabinet were convinced that America's Minister and military were supporting the insurgents. No matter what the purpose of the armed U.S. troops, their presence demoralized monarchy supporters and dampened any threat of violence.

In case of violence, everyone knew the Hawaiian Government's own military forces were no match for the better trained, better equipped U.S. forces.

If the Queen's troops had marched or fired on the Committee of Safety, it would have been impossible to avoid firing on the American troops. Yet Stevens informed Secretary of State John Foster: "...When the monarchy died by its own hand, there was no military force in the islands but the royal guard of about 75 natives, not an effective force equal to 20 American soldiers...."[27]

If this were true, then why were so many American soldiers called into action? Stevens wanted to dethrone the Queen.

The Kingdom Marshal, Charles Wilson, contradicted Stevens in a sworn affidavit, contending that there were 224 armed men at the Police Station.[28]

Dr. William Alexander, a historian and "reformer", wrote:

> To judge from their conduct, the Queen's Cabinet was
> overawed by the unanimity and determination of the for-
> eign community, and probably had an exaggerated idea of
> the force at the command of the Committee of Safety. They
> shrank from the responsibility of causing fruitless blood-
> shed, and sought a valid excuse for inaction, which they
> thought they found in the presence of the United States
> troops on shore, and in the well known sympathy of the
> American Minister with the opposition.[29]

O'ahu Governor A. Cleghorn immediately sent a letter to
Stevens protesting the American soldiers, but Stevens refused to
recall the troops.[30]

As the American soldiers marched along the downtown streets,
the Royal Hawaiian Band played its usual festive Monday night
concert under the outdoor gazebo at the Hawaiian Hotel, a few
blocks from 'Iolani Palace. Concert goers had no reason to
suspect that American troops were supporting a revolution. People
were used to seeing American soldiers, so no one expected
violence or revolution.

That evening, the Committee of Safety met again. Sanford
Dole, a man generally well-respected by all factions, including
annexationists and royalists, was invited to head the new government. Dole said he needed a day to think about it. He was not a
member of the Committee of Safety and had supported neither
overthrowing the monarchy, nor annexation. Dole preferred
replacing Queen Lili'uokalani with a regency favoring Princess
Ka'iulani, the Queen's designated heir.

Tuesday, January 17
The Queen Yields

This day, Sanford Dole agreed to accept the position as head
of Hawaii's new government.

The 18-member Provisional Government was dominated by 15 Americans or Hawaiian citizens of American origin, 5 of whom had drafted the 1887 Bayonet Constitution.[31] None were native Hawaiians.

Executive Council and Advisory Committee for the Anticipated Provisional Government [32]

Name	Citizenship	National Origin
Executive Council		
SB Dole (Chairman)	Hawai'i	Hawai'i-born American
JA King (Interior)	Hawai'i	American
PC Jones (Finance)	Hawai'i	American
WO Smith (Attorney General)	Hawai'i	Hawai'i-born American
Advisory Committee		
J Emmeluth	United States	American
WG Ashley	United States	American
ED Tenney	United States	American
FW McChesney	United States	American
JA McCandless	United States	American
FJ Wilhelm	United States	Hawai'i-born German
WC Wilder	Hawai'i	American
JF Morgan	Hawai'i	Hawai'i-born American
SM Damon	Hawai'i	Hawai'i-born American
WR Castle	Hawai'i	Hawai'i-born American
LA Thurston	Hawai'i	Hawai'i-born American
C Bolte	Hawai'i	German
H Waterhouse	Hawai'i	English
A Brown	England	Scotch

Some of the Queen's Cabinet members were invited to join the Committee of Safety's Executive Council, but none accepted.

About 2:00 p.m., Dole gave U.S. Minister Stevens a letter announcing that the Committee intended to abolish the monarchy. Dole recounts that Stevens said "I think you have a great opportunity."[33]

At no time, then or in later recorded accounts, did anyone suggest that U.S. Minister Stevens hesitated or cautioned the Committee about their intentions. Stevens knew in advance the Committee's plans, he told them what he would do, and advised them what they should do.

Thurston, in his memoirs, revealed that Stevens often let Thurston read official dispatches to the State Department.[34]

Dr. G. Trousseau, a prominent physician, disclosed: "Almost daily, to my personal knowledge, meetings were held at Mr. Stevens' house in which possibilities of a peaceful revolution with the prospects of annexation were discussed." These meetings were attended by Sanford Dole, Lorrin Thurston, Alfred Hartwell, Charles Carter and *U.S.S. Boston* Captain Gilbert Wiltse.[35]

Queen Lili'uokalani knew that the Committee of Safety was hurriedly recruiting men and arms for a possible violent confrontation, but she was more alarmed by the appearance of U.S. troops, backed by the American warship.

Queen Lili'uokalani tried to defuse the situation by publicly announcing that no new constitution would be offered for the time being. She also sent Stevens a personal note assuring him that the present constitution would be upheld.

When Stevens didn't reply, the Queen's Cabinet visited the American Legation (Stevens' home), at 2:45 p.m. and asked Stevens in person, if the United States had recognized a Provisional Government. Their message read:

> Her Hawaiian Majesty's Government having been informed that certain persons to them unknown have issued a proclamation declaring a Provisional Govern-

ment to exist in opposition to Her Majesty's Government, and have pretended to depose the Queen, her Cabinet and Marshal, and that certain treasonable persons at present occupy the Government Building in Honolulu with an armed force, and pretending that your excellency, in behalf of the United States of America, has recognized such Provisional Government, Her Majesty's Cabinet asks respectfully: has your excellency recognized said Provisional Government? and if not, Her Majesty's Government, under the above existing circumstances, respectfully requests the assistance of your Government in preserving the peace of the country.[36]

Stevens would not help the Queen.

At 3:10 p.m., he sent the Queen's Ministers a note from his second floor bedroom stating that he had already recognized the Provisional Government. After plotting the troop movement, renting Arion Hall, and meeting several times with the Committee of Safety, Stevens now took sick in the safety of his bed.

Coincidentally, illness also confined Lorrin Thurston to the sick bed this day.

Stevens' note was premature, and the Queen's Ministers were too late.

Before the Queen's Ministers traveled to Stevens' home – in fact, while they were still drafting the plea they would give to Stevens – a proclamation was being read by the Committee of Safety from the steps of the Government Building, about 75 yards from where American troops were stationed.[37]

Henry Cooper, an American citizen who had arrived in Hawai'i one year earlier, read the proclamation written by Lorrin Thurston, declaring that the Queen's Government had been overthrown. The proclamation announced that the monarchy no longer existed, and a new Provisional Government was established in its place, "to exist until terms of union with the United States of America have been negotiated and agreed upon."[38]

The insurgents immediately asked U.S. Minister Stevens to recognize them as the legitimate government. The insurgents didn't know it, but Stevens had already informed the Queen's Ministers that he had recognized the new government.

The first phase of the revolution was accomplished.

The Committee of Safety had become the Provisional Government.

The Provisional Government declared martial law, and sent messengers to request recognition from foreign diplomats in Honolulu.

An hour later, between 4:00-5:00 p.m. – before the Queen and her forces yielded – Stevens confirmed the insurgents' control of the Government Building, and sent a message to Dole giving de facto recognition of the Provisional Government. Again, Stevens acted prematurely. Some say it was a pre-planned "script", because Stevens later admitted that he had written the message earlier that afternoon and he "got the note ready without signing it beforehand."[39]

The brief acknowledgment read:

> United States Legation,
> Honolulu, January 17, 1893

> A Provisional Government having been duly constituted in the place of the recent Government of Queen Lili'uokalani and said Provisional Government being in full possession of the Government Building, the Archives and the Treasury and in control of the capital of the Hawaiian Islands, I hereby recognize said Provisional Government as the de facto government of the Hawaiian Islands.

> John Stevens,
> United States Minister[40]

Dole replied to Stevens:

> I acknowledge the receipt of your valued communication of this day, recognizing the Hawaiian Provisional Government, and express deep appreciation of the same.
>
> We have conferred with the Ministers of the late Government and have made demand upon the Marshal to surrender the station house. We are not actually yet in possession of the station house, but as night is approaching and our forces may be insufficient to maintain order, we request the immediate support of the United States forces, and would request that the commander of the United States forces take command of our military forces so that they may act together for the protection of the city.
>
> Sanford Dole[41]

As soon as the facts were known, it became evident that Stevens recognized the Provisional Government hastily and prematurely, because:

- the insurgents did not control the Police Station where most of the Queen's troops were stationed, and

- Queen Lili'uokalani and her Cabinet believed that the United States was supporting the insurgents.

Furthermore:

- Stevens recognized the Provisional Government as the de facto government before the Queen had yielded, and

- Stevens' reply to the Queen's Cabinet was delivered before Stevens sent his letter of recognition to the Provisional Government.

The timing of Stevens' letters undermined resistance by the Queen's Government, and strengthened the impression that American troops would protect the insurgents. Stevens tried, but failed to conceal that he had recognized the Provisional Government before the Queen yielded.

Members of the Provisional Government, backed by Stevens' support, called on the Queen, and demanded her abdication. The Queen protested, then yielded to the United States.

Her message to Dole contained a provisional surrender of the Kingdom's sovereignty:

> I, Lili'uokalani, by the Grace of God and under the Constitution of the Kingdom, Queen, do hereby solemnly protest against any and all acts done against myself and the constitutional Government of the Hawaiian Kingdom by certain persons claiming to have established a Provisional Government of and for this Kingdom.

> That I yield to the superior force of the United States of America, whose Minister Plenipotentiary, His Excellency John L. Stevens, has caused United States troops to be landed at Honolulu and declared that he would support the said Provisional Government.

> Now to avoid any collision of armed forces and perhaps the loss of life, I do under this protest, and impelled by said force, yield my authority until such time as the Government of the United States shall, upon the facts being presented to it, undo the action of its representatives and reinstate me in the authority which I claim as the constitutional sovereign of the Hawaiian Islands.

> Done at Honolulu this 17th day of January, A.D., 1893

> Lili'uokalani, R.[42]

**1893 Provisional Government (left to right): S. Damon,
J. King, S. Dole, H. Cooper, B. Marx, and W. Smith**

By yielding to the United States rather than to the Provisional
Government, Lili'uokalani expected that the United States would
help her regain her Kingdom, as England had done for Kamehameha
III, 50 years earlier, in 1843. Lili'uokalani nearly succeeded.

Dole signed his acceptance, implying concurrence with the
Queen's message, without realizing that she was only yielding her
throne temporarily – not abdicating.

In her autobiography, the Queen reiterated that she surrendered "in order to avoid bloodshed, and because I recognized the
futility of a conflict with so formidable a power (the United
States)."[43]

Lili'uokalani gave this account of January 17:

> ...At about 2:30 p.m., Tuesday, the establishment of
> the Provisional Government was proclaimed; and nearly
> 15 minutes later Mr. J. S. Walker came and told me 'that

1893 Provisional Government (left to right): J. King, S. Dole, W. Smith, and P. Jones . Note: There were many changes in the Provisional Government Cabinet

he had come on a painful duty, that the opposition party had requested that I should abdicate.' I told him that I had no idea of doing so...I immediately sent for (my Cabinet Ministers and advisors). The situation being taken into consideration, it was found that, since the troops of the United States had been landed to support the revolutionists, by the order of the American Minister, it would be impossible for us to make any resistance....[44]

At 7:00 p.m., the Police Station surrendered. A short time later, more than 200 Hawaiian soldiers gave up their arms.

American Flag is Raised

The next day, Stevens reported to Secretary of State Foster:

> All is quiet here now...Language can hardly express the enthusiasm and the profound feeling of relief at this peaceful and salutary change of government. The underlying cause of this profound feeling among the citizens is the hope that the United States Government will allow these Islands to pass to American control and become American soil.[45]

Lili'uokalani sent appeals to U.S. President Benjamin Harrison and to President-elect Grover Cleveland. To President Harrison she explained: "I submitted to force, believing that he (U.S. Minister Stevens) would not have acted in that manner unless by authority of the government which he represents."[46]

Lili'uokalani gave President Harrison three reasons why she surrendered her throne to the United States:

> The futility of a conflict with the United States, the desire to avoid violence and bloodshed and the destruction of life and property, and the certainty which I feel that you and your government will right whatever wrongs may have been inflicted upon us in the premises. [47]

To President-elect Cleveland she wrote: "...I leave our grievance in your hands, confident that in so far as you deem it proper we shall have your sympathy and your aid."[48]

Both the Queen and the Provisional Government rushed to plea their cause to American officials in Washington, D.C.

The Provisional Government immediately sought a treaty of annexation, while the Queen tried to delay any American decision until the events of her overthrow were investigated.

The Provisional Government and Lili'uokalani sent messages on the same ship. However, the Provisional Government forced the Queen to charter her own ship which carried her delegation of supporters two weeks later. Her attorney, Paul Neumann, took a petition signed by 3,400 voters opposed to the Provisional Government, which he submitted to the U.S. State Department.

Within two days, 14 nations recognized the Provisional Government: Germany, Austro-Hungary, Italy, Russia, Spain, Sweden, The Netherlands, Denmark, Belgium, Mexico, Chile, Peru, Great Britain and China.[49]

In the weeks to come, widespread rumors suggested that native Hawaiian supporters would try to regain power. The Provisional Government was not sufficiently stable, and lacked the military strength to insure its own existence. Again, American aid and support was sought and approved by U.S. Minister John Stevens.

On the last day of January, Stevens received a formal request to extend military protection to the Provisional Government pending treaty negotiations in Washington.

The next day, February 1, Stevens complied with that extraordinary request. He placed the Provisional Government under U.S. protection, and raised the American flag over Hawai'i. Stevens then sent Captain Wiltse of the *U.S.S. Boston* the following order:

> The Provisional Government of the Hawaiian Islands having...expressed...the fear that said government may be unable to protect life and property, and to prevent civil disorder in Honolulu...requests that the flag of the United States may be raised, for the protection of the Hawaiian Islands, and...confer on the United States, through the undersigned, freedom of occupation of the public building of the Hawaiian Government and the soil of the Hawaiian Islands, so far as may be necessary for the exercise of such protection, but not interfering with the administration of the public affairs, by said Provisional Government.

> I hereby ask you to comply with the spirit and terms of the request of the Hawaiian Provisional Government, and...to use all the force at your command, in the exercise of your best judgment and discretion, you and myself awaiting instructions from the United States Government at Washington.[50]

The raising of the American flag inspired insurgent historian W.D. Alexander to write: "Stevens was the right man for the crisis."[51]

The same day, Stevens sent three letters and a telegram to Secretary of State Foster, reporting that the Islands had been placed under United States protection. Stevens falsely wrote: "the Provisional Government of Hawai'i is gaining power and respect. Everything is quiet. Annexation sentiment is increasing."

Yet he also asked for permission to provide more permanent American troop protection. He expressed fear of danger if "renegade whites," "hoodlum foreigners," "vicious natives" and "evil-disposed persons might stir some of them (40,000 Chinese and Japanese) to disorder." Stevens also noted concerns about an arriving British warship.

Stevens' added these personal biases:

> ...Nearly all the Germans, the larger proportion of the respectable and responsible English, and almost the entire Portuguese population are warmly for annexation. This inclination of the Portuguese is quite important for they number seven or eight thousand, and are among the most industrious and saving...

Stevens described the annexation opponents as:

> ...the lower class of natives, led by unscrupulous foreigners, of little property, mostly from California, Australia, and Canada, who wish to maintain the Hawaiian monarchy and its corruptions for their own unworthy purposes, and who think their opportunities for power and spoliation will be gone if annexation becomes a fact....[52]

Now that the monarchy was overthrown, Stevens urged annexation rather than a protectorate, in this amazing message he sent to the State Department:

**1893 Annexation Committee to Washington, D.C.: (l-r)
Willliam Wilder, Joseph Marsden, Lorrin Thurston, Charles
Carter (standing), Dr. John Mott-Smith, William Castle**

The Hawaiian pear is now fully ripe, and this is the golden hour for the United States to pluck it. If annexation does not take place promptly or is held in doubt and suspense for six or seven months, there certainly will be a revulsion to despair, and these people by their necessities might be forced towards becoming a British colony, for the English here of the monarchical type would then avail themselves of their opportunity and stir up all possible opposition to annexation.

In his dispatch, Stevens reminded his superiors of former Secretary of State Marcy's $100,000 offer in 1854 to buy Hawai'i. Stevens suggested paying $150,000 for "liquidation" of all political claims: $70,000 each to former Queen Lili'uokalani and Crown Princess Ka'iulani, and $5,000 each to the brothers Kūhiō and Kawānanakoa, whom Stevens described as two "harmless young persons" made princes by King Kalākaua.

Stevens also wrote: "The old 'palace gang' for the past 10 days have been busy...getting signatures of natives...against annexation." He accused certain "renegade Americans" of "dirty work" and bribery.

In another message dated the same day, Stevens wrote: "with the islands under our protection we think the English Minister will not attempt to insist that his government has the right to interfere while our flag is over the Government Building."[53]

Officially, Secretary of State Foster commended and criticized Stevens' actions. Foster sent two messages to Stevens, on February 11 and 14, 1893. Foster approved using the soldiers, but disavowed the American protectorate and raising the U.S. flag.

Foster wrote:

> So far...as your action...at the request of...the de facto sovereign Government of the Hawaiian Islands, the co-operation of the...forces of the United States for the...protection of life and property from apprehended disorder, it is commended. But so far as it may appear to overstep that limit by setting the authority of the United States above that of the Government of the Hawaiian Islands, in the capacity of protector, or to impair in any way the independent sovereignty of the Hawaiian Government by substituting the flag and power of the United States..., it is disavowed.[54]

U.S. Secretary of State Foster allowed Stevens to keep the troops ashore as long as the soldiers did no more than preserve order, and protect American lives and property.

However, by the time Foster's message had confirmed Stevens' recognition of the Provisional Government, Queen Lili'uokalani had already surrendered to the United States – making the Provisional Government the legitimate government, as far as the Harrison Administration was concerned.

When newspapers in the United States received word about the overthrow, the reaction varied. For example, headlines in several New York newspapers ranged from the *New York World:* "Hawaii is free. Lili Upsets the Constitution and is Herself Overthrown"; the *New York Sun:* "Hawaii Asks to Come in. Revolution Successful, She Seeks Annexation"; and the *New York Herald:* "Minister Stevens Helped Overthrow Lili".[55]

New York Herald news reporter Charles Nordhoff referred to Hawai'i as "stolen property." He informed newspaper readers:

> We in America have not the least objection to your revolution if you do it yourselves. What we dislike is that you got the United States troops to help you and made yourselves the rulers of the islands. Then you began to cry for annexation and hastened to Washington to get us to take off your hands what was then your stolen property.[56]

President Benjamin Harrison now had just one month left to his term, which didn't allow enough time to get Congress to ratify an annexation treaty. On February 3, President Harrison admitted, "I am sorry the Hawaiian question did not come six months sooner or 60 days later, as it is embarrassing to begin without the time to finish."[57]

Thurston told Dole on February 9:

> He (U.S. Secretary of State Foster) informed us on Thursday that he was instructed by the President to say that the President and Cabinet had made up their minds to annex the Islands; that they were willing to do so on as nearly the lines that we asked as was possible...They have made up their minds to act immediately....[58]

Despite the time constraint, the Harrison Administration quickly negotiated an annexation treaty, which the President sent to the U.S. Senate on February 15, just one month after the overthrow. President Harrison tried to rush the treaty through the Senate, while at the same time, denying American involvement in overthrowing the Hawaiian monarchy.

On this day, Secretary of State John Foster reminded President Harrison: "...Annexation has been on more than one occasion avowed as a policy and attempted as a fact."[59]

President Harrison urged the Senate to give "prompt action" to the annexation treaty. He said:

> The overthrow of the monarchy was not in any way promoted by this Government... and the change of government in the Hawaiian Islands...was entirely unexpected so far as the United States was concerned. The change was in fact abrupt and unlooked-for by the United States Minister or the Naval Commander.[60]

On March 1, two Japanese warships steamed into Honolulu Harbor, followed soon after by a British warship. Stevens hurriedly telegraphed Secretary of State Foster: "It is advisable to send here at once the most powerful American ship available."[61]

Stevens charged that the new Japanese Commissioner would demand political rights for Japanese plantation workers and would have tried to take control of Hawai'i if the United States hadn't acted first.

In-coming President Grover Cleveland, an anti-expansionist Democrat, would occupy the White House on March 4, 1893. Cleveland was America's only President to serve two non-consecutive terms, from 1885-1889 and 1893-1897.

Historians credit President Cleveland as man of integrity. For example, back in 1885, he withdrew from the U.S. Senate a pending treaty authorizing the construction of a canal through Nicaragua, linking the Atlantic and Pacific Oceans. He also withdrew pending reciprocity treaties with the Dominican Republic and Spain.[62]

Once in the White House, President Cleveland opposed the annexation of Hawai'i, and withdrew the treaty from the Senate "for the purpose of re-examination."[63]

America's Dilemma

"...The Provisional Government owes its existence to
an armed invasion by the United States. By an act of war...a
substantial wrong has been done."
—U.S. President Grover Cleveland

"We have always extended the privilege of interference in the domestic policy of Hawai'i."
—U.S. Senator John Morgan (D-Alabama)

The Blount Report

Two months after President Cleveland's 1893 inauguration,
the bubble of economic prosperity burst. The "Panic of 1893" hit
America hard, caused by over speculation, bad loans, and the
corrupt business trusts and monopolies of the "Robber Baron" era.
Thousands of businesses failed, banks and railroads filed bankruptcy, and unemployment shot upward. America fell $70
million into debt.[1]

President Cleveland devoted most of his attention in a belea-
guered second term fighting this severe national depression, one
of the most disastrous in American history.

He had much more to worry about than Hawai'i.

Nevertheless, the President dedicated considerable energy to
achieving an honest and fair solution to the "Hawai'i problem."
For his efforts, President Cleveland received both praise and
ridicule from politicians, the press, and the public.

Almost immediately after taking office, President Cleveland
sent former U.S. Congressman James Blount (D-Georgia) on a
fact-finding mission to Hawai'i to investigate the American
participation in the overthrow of the monarchy.

Blount had just retired after serving 18 years in the U.S. House

of Representatives (1873-1893), including a term as chairman of the
House Committee on Foreign Affairs. He was well-informed about
international affairs and respected
by colleagues of both political parties. Blount had no obvious view on
annexation prior to his appointment.

At first, Blount did not want to be
the U.S. Minister to Hawai'i, but the
official title made it easier to carry
out the duties the President assigned
to him. Blount intended his mission
to be a temporary assignment.

Blount arrived in Hawai'i on
March 29, 1893, and relieved U.S.
Minister John Stevens on May 24.

"Paramount Blount", as he was
nicknamed during his four month
tenure in Hawai'i, received sweep-
ing instructions:

James Blount

> ...Your authority in all matters...is paramount...(You
> have) full discretion and power to determine when (mili-
> tary) forces should be landed or withdrawn. [2]

Blount took great care to preserve his impartiality. He told no
one his personal feelings, and gave no newspaper interviews. For
keeping his mouth closed, he was known in Hawai'i as the
"Minister reticent." The *San Francisco Chronicle* newspaper
called him an "oyster-like diplomat."[3] Blount recognized that
each side – the Queen and the new Provisional Government –
had a desperate case to present.

The American flag still waved over Honolulu, and American
troops continued to march on Honolulu streets when Blount arrived.

It didn't take Blount long to learn the truth about the roles of Stevens, Wiltse, and U.S. troops in dethroning the Queen.

During his entire assignment, Blount expressed concern that many people refused to believe that he would be impartial. After the biased John Stevens, it wasn't surprising that native Hawaiians distrusted American diplomats. On April 8, Blount wrote to new U.S. Secretary of State Walter Gresham, a Republican-turned Democrat, and a retired Federal Judge:

> ...The existing (Provisional) Government owes its being and its maintenance to this perverted influence...it is not easy for me to impress persons here with the complete idea of our noninterference policy....[4]

Pau

Rear Admiral Joseph Skerrett relieved the portly Captain Gilbert Wiltse, who completed his tour of duty in February, 1893. Wiltse retired from a 38-year Navy career, and died in New York a few months later.

U.S. Minister John Stevens, now 73 years old, submitted his resignation letter on March 7. He would have been removed by the Democratic Cleveland Administration anyway. In his last days as U.S. Minister, he defended his actions to the new Secretary of State Walter Gresham:

> Had the United States Minister and Naval Commander not acted as they did, they would have de served prompt removal from their places and the just censure of the friends of humanity and civilization.[5]

Stevens returned to Maine. He wrote and lectured in defense of his well-publicized actions in Hawai'i. He died in 1895.

Blount waited three days until April 1 – so as not to act in haste – then he lowered the American flag, and ordered an end to Stevens' two month protectorate.

He also terminated America's military occupation of Hawai'i by ordering the remaining American soldiers out of the Government Building, and back to the *U.S.S. Boston.*

Blount conducted an extensive investigation by speaking informally with people, then asking some to submit written statements and affidavits. He took depositions with accuracy and candor.

The Provisional Government gave Blount a long list of people to interview, which he rejected. Blount said he would listen to all who wished to be heard. Key officials of the Provisional Government were asked for interviews or statements, but most refused. Their refusal to cooperate – intended as a response to Blount's investigation methods and his lowering of the American flag – hindered Blount's fact-finding mission.

Blount interviewed 60 royalists and 20 annexationists – including five members of the Provisional Government, two members of the Committee of Safety, one Executive Council member, three Advisory Council members, and two of the speakers at the annexationists' January 16, 1893 mass meeting.[6]

Blount interviewed Committee of Safety member, William O. Smith (Lorrin Thurston's law partner), who submitted a written statement with fellow Committee members Henry Cooper and William Castle. He also interviewed Samuel Damon and former U.S. Minister John Stevens.

In time, the Provisional Government would criticize Blount for interviewing too many royalists and too few insurgents. Some complained that testimonies were slanted in the final report.

Blount also interviewed Stevens, who admitted that he had "recognized the Provisional Government before the barracks and station house had been surrendered." Stevens told Blount he did not "consider their surrender of any importance."[7]

Blount first became suspicious of former Minister Stevens

when Stevens tried to persuade him not to lower the flag or recall the troops. Stevens brought Walter Smith, editor of an annexationist newspaper, the *Honolulu Star,* to warn Blount about rumors that a Japanese warship in Honolulu harbor would land troops to restore the Queen's authority.[8]

Blount became even more suspicious when, on two occasions, he asked Stevens for important documents that Stevens said he couldn't find: his communication from the Committee of Safety asking for American troops to land, and his communication recognizing the Provisional Government.

Blount reported to U.S. Secretary of State Gresham on May 6:

> Mr. Stevens seemed to be at a loss as to whether he had such a paper. This same difficulty occurred when I called upon him for the communication from the Committee of Safety asking for the landing of the troops of the *Boston.*[9]

Everyone wondered anxiously what the tight-lipped Blount would report to the President.

Blount departed for Washington on August 9. His lengthy, 700-page report blamed U.S. Minister John Stevens for the overthrow of the monarchy. Blount charged that *U.S.S. Boston* troops had landed under false pretenses, not to protect American lives and property, but to aid in overthrowing the monarchy.

In his official report, Blount chose his words carefully. He concluded that Stevens and Wiltse were guilty of "complicity" by failing to discourage the insurgents from seeking to overthrow the Queen and substitute a Provisional Government.[10]

Blount pointed out: "In less than 30 hours the (insurgents) have overturned the throne, established a new government, and obtained the recognition of foreign powers."

Furthermore, "That a deep wrong has been done the Queen and the native race by American officials pervades the native mind and that of the Queen, as well as a hope for redress from the United States, there can be no doubt."[11]

Blount recommended restoring the former monarchy.

He reported, "American citizens here have been the most active in dethroning the Queen...."[12] He identified Thurston, an American missionary descendant, as "the leading spirit" of the insurgency.[13]

Blount said the insurgency had been planned long before the Queen tried to proclaim a new constitution. He charged:

> The letters of the American Minister and naval officers stationed at Honolulu in 1892 indicate that any failure to appoint a ministry of the Reform Party would produce a political crisis. The voting out of the (George) Wilcox Cabinet...had more to do with the revolution than the Queen's proclamation. The first was the foundation – the latter the opportunity.[14]

Blount's report also said: "The American Minister and the revolutionary leaders had determined on annexation to the United States, and had agreed on the part each was to act to the very end..."[15]

He added, "The undoubted sentiment of the people is for the Queen, against the Provisional Government, and against annexation."[16]

Blount chronicled these activities:

> Mr. Stevens consulted freely with the leaders of the revolutionary movement from the evening of the 14th. These disclosed to him all their plans. They feared arrest and punishment. He promised them protection. They needed troops...to overawe the Queen's supporters and government. This he agreed to, and did furnish. They had few arms and no trained soldiers. They did not mean to fight. It was arranged between them and the American Minister that the proclamation dethroning the Queen and organizing a Provisional Government should be read from the Government Building and he would follow it with a speedy recognition...with American troops...and artillery

(located) within a stone's throw (from the Government Building).

> The leaders of the revolutionary movement would not have undertaken it but for Mr. Stevens' promise to protect them against any danger from the government. Had the troops not been landed, no measure for the organization of a new Government would have been taken.

He added: "The Queen (believed)...the President would restore her crown" as England had restored the Kingdom to King Kamehameha III after it was taken by George Paulet in 1843, and the British Government "obtained full information." [17]

Blount wrote, England's historic decision to restore the Kingdom sovereignty "made a deep impression" on the Queen and her advisers. The Queen's advisors were confident that the actions of Wiltse and Stevens "would be repudiated by the United States Government and that she could appeal to it."[18]

Blount commented on the racial prejudices which preoccupied people in Hawai'i: "The important offices were held by white men...They sought to succeed to the political control exercised by their fathers (the missionaries)."[19]

For example, Samuel Damon, a descendant of American missionaries, said:

> It is the clashing of two nationalities for supremacy...the Hawaiian is thinking, because he had a majority of votes, that it gave him power. He didn't recognize that the intelligent and strong will of the Anglo-Saxon would beat him every time.[20]

Blount tried honestly to report the feelings of American "reformers" living in Hawai'i, when he wrote "The native is unfit for government and his power must be curtailed."[21]

Blount noted:

There is not an annexationist in the islands, so far as I have been able to observe, who would be willing to submit the question of annexation to a popular vote. Annexationists insist upon restricting the native vote to leave political power in the hands of the whites.[22]

When the Committee of Safety walked to the Government Building to read its revolutionary proclamation, Blount reported, "there was no sign of an insurrectionary soldier on the street." Only later did about 30-40 insurgent soldiers appear.[23]

Across the street, however, American troops stationed at Arion Hall occupied "an armed position on the principal square of the town commanding the Palace and the Government Building."[24] These troops were "located to suggest to the Queen and her counselors" that American troops were cooperating with the insurrection, and "when the emergency arose" would provide "active support."[25]

Blount explained:

If the Queen's troops should have attacked the Provisional Government troops our men were in danger of being injured, which might have brought them into collision with the Queen's troops. The same is true if the Provisional Government troops advanced on the Palace. If American troops were landed to protect American property and the persons of American citizens, their location at this place, unfortunately, signified a different purpose.

The Queen, her Cabinet, and her followers undoubtedly believed from the location of the American troops and the quick recognition of the Provisional Government by Mr. Stevens, that the United States forces would aid the Provisional Government forces in the event of a conflict.

Blount added:

The request of the Committee of Safety on which the landing of the troops was made, did not ask for the protection of the property and persons of American citizens. [26]

Blount drew these conclusions because Stevens had privately told the Committee of Safety that he would recognize them when they occupied the Government Building, and the Committee of Safety read their proclamation from the steps of that building. Blount declared:

A building was chosen where there were no troops stationed, where there was no struggle to be made to obtain access...More than this − before any demand for surrender had even been made on the Queen or on the commander or any officer of any of her military forces at any of the points where her troops were located, the American Minister had recognized the Provisional Government and was ready to give it the support of the United States troops! [27]

Blount also interviewed Queen Lili'uokalani. She denounced:

• the missionaries and their children

• the "interference" of Stevens for his "conspiring" actions which have "placed me and my people in this unhappy position" and

• United States troops

The Queen defended her attempt to proclaim a new constitution as "an answer to the prayers and petitions of my people."

She maintained that the 1887 Bayonet Constitution didn't prohibit her from proclaiming a new constitution. She denied that her attempted constitution was "a revolutionary act."

"My Cabinet encouraged me," Lili'uokalani told Blount, "then afterwards advised me to the contrary." After yielding, she asked, why did the Government continue "making preparations for war....?"[28]

The Queen asked why American troops were necessary:

> Why had they landed when everything was at peace? I was told that it was for the safety of American citizens and the protection of their interests. Then why had they not gone to the residences, instead of drawing in line in front of the Palace gates, with guns pointed at us?[29]

Lili'uokalani appealed to Blount, hoping that the United States "will restore to me and to my nation all the rights that have been taken away by the action of her Minister" and to have the "independent stand amongst the civilized nations of the world" restored to her Kingdom.[30]

U.S. Secretary of State Walter Gresham carefully read Blount's report, and agreed with it. Gresham advised President Cleveland not to resubmit the annexation treaty to the Senate. He also recommended doing something to restore the Queen and her government.

Deport the Queen?

As Blount was finalizing his report against the Provisional Government, its diplomat in Washington, Lorrin Thurston, was working diligently to negotiate an annexation treaty. Thurston met with U.S. Secretary of State Gresham. From this and other meetings, Thurston learned about President Cleveland's dilemma. He apprised Hawai'i Provisional Government President Sanford Dole in a confidential June 13 letter:

"Mr. Gresham told me the simple truth when he said that the President did not know what he is going to do."

In that same letter, Thurston recommended deporting Lili'uokalani:

As long as she remains (in Hawai'i) she forms a rallying center around which all malcontents will gather, and would be especially dangerous in the contingency of any outbreak occurring. It is certainly an unheard of thing to allow a deposed sovereign to remain in the country after deposition...and to make open and continuous claim to the throne and actively work therefor.

Thurston objected to the possibility of Hawai'i becoming a crown colony of England.

It seems to me it is the United States or nothing...and that if we cannot get annexation now, the best thing to do is to hang on at all hazards...until we secure what we want from them or the succeeding administration. [31]

Smith wrote to his law partner Thurston about "the plotting and scheming among the low foreign element...some fear trouble. There will be no peace here, or freedom from revolutionary schemes until we come under the U.S."[32]

In mid-summer, the Hawaiian Patriotic League gave President Cleveland a massive petition with 7,500 signatures against annexation.[33]

Despite the widespread native Hawaiian support for the Queen, Thurston wrote to Dole in late 1893 that he was confident the United States would not seek a military solution:

I am reliably informed that (Secretary of State) Gresham has within a few days stated that under no circumstances would the United States undertake to support the Queen by force, once she was back.[34]

Did the Queen Say "Beheading"?

Gresham expressed these concerns about Hawai'i in a letter to Carl Schurz, a prominent American magazine editor:

I can say to you in confidence that if anything can be
established by proof, Mr. Blount's reports show that the
action of the American Minister and the presence of the
United States troops in Honolulu overawed the Queen –
put her in fear – and induced her to abdicate and surrender
to the so-called Provisional Government, with the understanding however, that her case would be fairly considered
by the President of the United States. Should not this great
wrong be undone? 'Yes,' I say decidedly. [35]

In another letter, Gresham said he "oppose(d) taking the
Islands by force and fraud."[36]

U.S. Attorney General Richard Olney was less inclined as
Gresham to recommend strong presidential action. Olney felt the
United States couldn't undo what already had been done, so he
urged the President not to send in the troops to restore the Queen.
Olney wanted Congress to decide if force was necessary.

Olney, who would replace Gresham as Secretary of State two
years later, convinced the President that Lili'uokalani must grant
a full pardon to the officers of the Provisional Government.

The Attorney General said that any efforts to restore the
Queen would involve "practical difficulties."

Olney confessed:

A greater outrage upon a weak nation by a strong one
could hardly be imagined. If, however, the question is
whether having been wrongfully dethroned by the United
States, she can properly be re-enthroned by the same
power, the matter is a much more complex one.... [37]

In considering Blount's recommendations, and the advice of
Gresham and Olney, the idealistic President Cleveland sent Albert
Willis as the new Minister to Hawai'i, with high hopes and orders
to apologize to Lili'uokalani for Stevens' poor conduct. Willis
would tell the Queen that President Cleveland wanted to help her.

Willis, a former county attorney in Kentucky, had served in

Congress from 1877-1887. Secretary of State Gresham instructed Willis to:

Albert Willis

> ...Inform the Queen...the President's sincere regret that the reprehensible conduct of the American Minister (Stevens) and the unauthorized presence on land of a military force of the United States obliged her to surrender her sovereignty, for the time being, and rely on the justice of this Government to undo the flagrant wrong. [38]

When the Queen is reinstated, Gresham advised Willis, "the President expects that she will...grant full amnesty to all who participated in the movement against her...." The Provisional Government, Gresham added, is "expected to promptly relinquish to her constitutional authority."[39]

Willis arrived in Hawai'i on November 4, 1893. He interviewed Lili'uokalani nine days later at his residence, supposedly alone and in private. Yet behind a screen, in the adjacent room, Willis' stenographer took notes of the conversation. Lili'uokalani was suspicious.

The Queen did not know that the fate of her monarchy rested with this interview.

U.S. Minister Willis reported:

> I then said to her, 'the President expects and believes that when reinstated, you will show forgiveness and magnanimity, that you will wish to be the Queen of all the people, both native and foreign-born, that you will make

haste to secure their love and loyalty and to establish peace, friendship, and good government.' To this, she made no reply.

After waiting a moment, I continued: 'The President not only tenders you his sympathy but wishes to help you. Before fully making known to you, his purposes, I desire to know, whether you are willing to answer certain questions which it my duty to ask.' She answered, 'I am willing.'

I then asked her, 'Should you be restored to the throne, would you grant full amnesty as to life and property to all persons who have been instrumental in overthrowing your government.' She hesitated a moment and then slowly and calmly answered: 'There are certain laws of my government by which I shall abide. My decision would be, as the law directs, that such persons should be beheaded and their property confiscated to the government.'

I then said, repeating very distinctly her words, 'It is your feeling that these people should be beheaded and their property confiscated?' She replied, 'It is.' I then said to her, 'Do you fully understand the meaning of every word which I have said to you and of every word which you have said to me, and if so do you still have the same opinion?' Her answer was, 'I have understood and mean all I have said, but I might leave the decision of this to my Ministers.'

To this I replied, 'Suppose it was necessary to make a decision before you appointed any Ministers and that you were asked to issue a royal proclamation of general amnesty, would you do it?' She answered, 'I have no legal right to do that and I would not do it...They must be sent out of the country or punished and their property confiscated.'[40]

The Queen's statements shocked and confused Willis about his diplomatic assignment, so he asked Secretary of State Gresham for further instructions. Gresham telegraphed this reply on December 3:

> Should the Queen refuse assent to the written conditions, you will at once inform her that the President will cease interposition in her behalf, and that while he deems it his duty to endeavor to restore to the sovereign the constitutional government of the islands, his further efforts in that direction will depend upon the Queen's unqualified agreement...(against) punishment for what has been done in the past by those setting up or supporting the Provisional Government...The President (is acting) under dictates of honor and duty.[41]

Gresham added:

> ...It would not be just to put one party at the mercy of another. Should the Queen ask whether, if she accedes to conditions, active steps will be taken by the United States to effect her restoration, or to maintain her authority thereafter, you will say that the President can not use force without the authority of Congress.[42]

Willis' visits with Queen Lili'uokalani made the Provisional Government nervous. Rumors spread quickly. Would American soldiers return Lili'uokalani to the throne by attacking the Provisional Government? It didn't help matters that Willis, like Blount, did not reveal the purpose of his mission to people in Hawai'i.

This secrecy prompted 150 Americans in Hawai'i to submit a protest letter to U.S. Admiral Irwin in early December, warning that the United States would be "held responsible" if any possible act of war or hostility "were taken, attempted or announced in the time of profound peace now existing between the United States and the Hawaiian Islands."[43]

Because of the tense situation, and to maintain secrecy, Willis sent and received messages to Washington in naval code. Willis complained that the coded messages confused him.

Gresham became increasingly disturbed with Willis' dispatches, so he sent Willis this message:

> The brevity and uncertainty of your telegrams are embarrassing. You will insist upon amnesty and recognition of obligation of the Provisional Government as essential conditions of restoration. All interests will be promoted by prompt action. [44]

Willis began to doubt the practicality of restoring and maintaining Lili'uokalani in her former position.[45] He raised these issues in a confidential dispatch to Gresham on December 9:

> Assuming the restoration of the Queen with the temporary acquiescence of the Provisional Government and its supporters, what next? If left to itself, under existing conditions, it would fall to pieces like a card house. Would it be just to restore her and have another revolution at once – which seems probable. If restored would she not be entitled to our protection until she was securely seated? How long would this require.

Willis continued:

> From 1840 up to the Queen's dethronement the American power behind the throne was greater than the throne, filling (Hawaii's) judgeships, missions, Cabinets and Legislatures, and dominating the policy of the country. Whether this paramount influence can be revived is questionable. An examination of the Constitution of 1887 will disclose how this (American) colony so numerically has ruled the islands.' [46]

Willis confidentially admitted to Gresham that he was "surprised and disappointed" with the Queen's response. He gave her "several opportunities to modify or withdraw her demands."[47]

Willis interviewed Lili'uokalani two more times, on December 16 and 18. In his second interview, Willis read to the Queen her previous statement, as it was recorded by a stenographer, in which Lili'uokalani allegedly spoke the word, "beheading". Lili'uokalani replied, "That is a form of punishment which has never been used in the Hawaiian Islands, either before or since the coming of foreigners."

After reading in American newspapers that she advocated the beheading punishment, Lili'uokalani said she felt "horror" because it was untrue. Moreover, she assumed her interview with Willis was confidential. She didn't know a stenographer was hiding behind the screen, taking notes in the next room.

The Queen, in her autobiography (published five years later, in 1898), denied saying anything about beheading.

On the contrary, Lili'uokalani said she told Willis: "As to granting amnesty, it was beyond my powers...Our laws read that those who are guilty of treason should suffer the penalty of death."

She explained, "I would be more inclined personally to punish them by banishment, and confiscation of their property to the government." Lili'uokalani repeated several times that she must consult with her Ministers before deciding on any definite action.

Lili'uokalani said: the people of the Provisional Government had committed their second offense, the first being the forcing of the Bayonet Constitution on Kalākaua. She added:

> Their very residence would be a constant menace; that there never would be peace in my country, or harmony...as long as such a disturbing element remained, especially after they had once been successful in seizing the reins of government.[48]

U.S. troops parade at Honolulu wharf with
***USS Philadelphia* docked in the harbor (1895)**

Willis met with Lili'uokalani a third time, on December 18. She withdrew the death penalty for permanently exiling the insurgents and confiscating their property. Then, a few hours later, Lili'uokalani notified Willis by letter that she would agree to a full pardon and amnesty without any punishment.

The American public was outraged by the Queen's desire for bloodthirsty revenge, even though the death penalty may be imposed in the United States as a punishment for treason[49] and capital punishment is permissible in many states.

That same day, five thousand miles from Honolulu, U.S. Secretary of State Walter Gresham made a final effort to convince President Cleveland to help the Hawaiian Queen:

> Should not the great wrong done to a feeble but independent State by an abuse of the authority of the United States be undone by restoring the legitimate government? Anything short of that will not, I respectfully

A crowd watches U.S. Marines scale an 8 foot wall fronting Kawaiaha'o Church

submit, satisfy the demands of justice.[50]

The troops were landed not to protect American life and property, but to aid in overthrowing the existing government.[51]

Gresham's last gasp effort failed.

As fate – and timing – would have it, Queen Lili'uokalani's capitulation to President Cleveland's demand for full pardon came too late. On this day, the President announce his position to Congress, and to the people of America and Hawai'i.

President Cleveland's Dilemma

Finding himself at an impasse with both the Provisional Government and Queen Lili'uokalani, President Cleveland reported his findings to Congress on December 18, 1893, in a historically momentous speech which acknowledged America's guilt:[52]

> There is as little basis for the pretense that (American) forces were landed for the security of American life and property. When these armed men were landed, the city of Honolulu was in its customary orderly and peaceful condition. There was no symptom or disturbance in any quarter. Men, women, and children were about the streets as usual, and nothing varied the ordinary routine or disturbed the ordinary tranquillity, except the landing of the *Boston's* marines, and their march through the town.

> Thus it appears that Hawai'i was taken possession of by the United States forces without the consent or wish of the Government of the islands, or of anybody else so far as shown, except the United States Minister.

> The United States Minister, pursuant to prior agreement, recognized this (Provisional) Government within an hour after the reading of the proclamation (by an American citizen)...

> Therefore the military occupation of Honolulu by the United States...was wholly without justification...The Provisional Government owes its existence to an armed invasion by the United States.

> The United States had allied itself with her enemies, had recognized them as the true Government of Hawai'i, and had put her and her adherents in the position of opposition against lawful authority.

> ...The lawful Government of Hawai'i was overthrown without the drawing of a sword or the firing of a shot by a process every step of which, it may safely be asserted, is

directly traceable to and dependent for its success upon the agency of the United States acting through its diplomatic and naval representatives.

President Cleveland called attention to U.S. Minister Stevens' overt activities to support the overthrow:

But for the notorious predilections of the United States Minister for Annexation, the Committee of Safety, which should be called the Committee for Annexation, would never have existed.

But for the landing of the United States forces upon false pretexts respecting the danger to life and property the Committee would never have exposed themselves to the plans and penalties of treason by undertaking the subversion of the Queen's Government.

But for the presence of the United States forces in the immediate vicinity and in position to afford all needed protection and support the Committee would not have proclaimed the Provisional Government from the steps of the Government Building.

And finally, but for the lawless occupation of Honolulu under the false pretexts by the United States forces, and but for Minister Stevens' recognition of the Provisional Government when the United States forces were its sole support and constituted its only military strength, the Queen and her government would never have yielded to the Provisional Government, even for a time and for the sole purpose of submitting her case to the enlightened justice of the United States.

President Cleveland described the United States military demonstration as:

...An act of war, unless made either with the consent of the Government of Hawai'i or for the bona fide purpose of protecting the imperiled lives and property of citizens of the United States. But there is no pretense of any such consent on the part of the Government of the Queen, which at that time was undisputed and was both the de facto and de jure Government.

...The one controlling factor in the whole affair was unquestionably the United States Marines, who, drawn up under arms and with artillery in readiness...

President Cleveland called attention to "the extraordinary haste" connected with the Hawaiian annexation treaty:

...Our country was in danger of occupying the position of having actually set up a temporary government on foreign soil for the purpose of acquiring through that agency territory which we had wrongfully put in its possession. The control of both sides of a bargain acquired in such a manner is called by familiar name when found in private transactions.

President Cleveland accused U.S. Minister Stevens of misleading the former President and Congress, and charged him with:

The hasty recognition of a government openly and concededly set up for the purpose of tendering to us territorial annexation.

While naturally sympathizing with every effort to establish a republican form of government, it has been the settled policy of the United States to concede to people of foreign countries the same freedom and independence in the management of their domestic affairs that we have always claimed for ourselves, and it has been our practice to recognize revolutionary governments as soon as it became apparent that they were supported by the people.

For illustration of this rule I need only to refer to the revolution in Brazil in 1889, when our Minister was instructed to recognize the Republic 'so soon as a majority of the people of Brazil should have signified their assent to its establishment and maintenance;' to the revolution in Chile, in 1891, when our Minister was directed to recognize the new government 'if it was accepted by the people,' and to the revolution in Venezuela in 1892, when our recognition was accorded on condition that the new government was 'fully established, in possession of the power of the nation, and accepted by the people...'

President Cleveland pointed out that:

The Provisional Government has not assumed a republic or other constitutional form, but has remained a mere executive council or oligarchy, set up without the assent of the people. Indeed, the representatives of that government assert that the people of Hawai'i are unfit for popular government and frankly avow that they can be best ruled by arbitrary or despotic power.

The...Provisional Government and their supporters...have been led to their present predicament of revolt against the Government of the Queen by the indefensible encouragement and assistance of our diplomatic representative.

It did not appear that such Provisional Government had the sanction of either popular revolution or suffrage.

President Cleveland concluded:

The (overthrow) was one which was zealously promoted by the Minister representing the United States. He evidently had the ardent desire that it should become a fact accomplished...during his Ministry, and was not inconveniently scrupulous as to the means employed to that end.

...(I)f a feeble but friendly state is in danger of being robbed of its independence and its sovereignty by a misuse of the name and power of the United States, the United States can not fail to vindicate its honor and its sense of justice by an earnest effort to make all possible reparation....

Two days after the Queen's amnesty decision and President Cleveland's historic message to Congress, Willis met with the Provisional Government on December 20.

Speaking for the President, Willis acknowledged that the United States had committed a wrong, and asked Hawai'i President Sanford Dole to resign and to restore the Kingdom Government.

Willis said:

Upon the facts embodied in Mr. Blount's reports, the President has arrived at certain conclusions and determined upon a certain course of action with which it becomes my duty to acquaint you.

The Provisional Government was not established by the Hawaiian people or with their consent or acquiescence, nor has it since existed with their consent...

...I have secured the Queen's agreement...to grant full amnesty to all who participated in the movement against her...

In the name and by the authority of the United States of America, I submit to you the question, 'Are you willing to abide by the decision of the President?'[53]

Rather than press for an immediate response as he did with the Queen, Willis allowed Dole three days to prepare a formal answer. President Dole needed the time. He anxiously awaited the arrival of a ship bringing news of Congressional attitudes toward President Cleveland's Hawaiian policy. That same ship was carrying an important passenger, Lorrin Thurston, the Provisional Government's chief propagandist, on his return from Washington.

Thurston probably advised his Provisional Government that the United States would not try to return the Queen to power by military means. He also helped to write Dole's 50-page blunt response to Minister Willis, sent on December 23:

> If the American forces illegally assisted the revolution in the establishment of the Provisional Government, that Government is not responsible for their wrong-doing. It was purely a private matter for discipline between the United States Government and its own officers.[54]

Dole said the Provisional Government didn't recognize President Cleveland's right to interfere in its affairs, that the United States and other nations had recognized the Provisional Government as Hawaii's legitimate government, that the revolution would have occurred with or without the U.S. soldiers. Finally, Dole added that the Provisional Government wasn't responsible for what the American soldiers had done.

On January 12, 1894, Gresham sent to Willis a final dispatch of President Cleveland's disappointment with the Provisional Government's decision:

> The President sincerely regrets that the Provisional Government refuses to acquiesce in the conclusion which his sense of right and duty and a due regard for our national honor constrained him to reach and submit as a measure of justice to the people of the Hawaiian Islands and their deposed sovereign...The subversion of the Hawaiian Government by an abuse of the authority of the United States was in plain violation of international law and required the President to disavow and condemn the act of our offending

officials, and, within the limits of his constitutional power,
to endeavor to restore the lawful authority. [55]

One month after President Cleveland's historic speech, the
Provisional Government celebrated its first anniversary. The
Hawaiian Star newspaper reported the anniversary celebration
in a January 18 story, with a headline: "A good word for Mr.
Willis". The newspaper story reported: "...He (Willis) was
instructed to do a difficult job. 'Don't use force, but don't let them
(Provisional Government) know that you won't use it.'"[56]

Thurston and the Provisional Government leaders reasoned,
if President Cleveland hadn't acted to restore the Queen after one
year, he probably wouldn't try now.

And that's what happened. The President admitted his good-
will policy had failed, and he had done all he could do.

The President dumped the problem in the lap of Congress.

For several months, Congress debated and argued about
Hawai'i without reaching a consensus. The House passed one
resolution, and the Senate passed another.

The pro-expansionist Republicans in the House were voted
down on a resolution amendment urging eventual annexation of
Hawai'i.   Then the Republicans tried to censure Democratic
President Cleveland for his efforts to restore the monarchy, but the
resolution failed by a vote of 103 to 159, with 89 abstentions.[57]

Finally, on February 7, 1894, the U.S. House of Representatives voted 177 to 78, with 96 abstentions, to condemn former U.S.
Minister Stevens. The short, two-paragraph resolution charged
that Stevens' actions were "contrary to the traditions of our
Republic and the spirit of our constitution, and should be condemned."

The House Resolution cited Stevens for his role in "illegally
aiding" the overthrow of Hawaii's legitimate government. In
addition, the resolution opposed the annexation of Hawai'i or
making the islands an American protectorate. The resolution,
sponsored by Congressman James McCreary (D-Kentucky) pro-

claimed: "interference with the domestic affairs of an independent nation is contrary to the spirit of American institutions." [58]

That second part of the resolution prevented the Cleveland Administration from sending in troops to restore the deposed Queen. The large number of abstaining votes indicates that many Congressmen were not comfortable that two separate issues were combined into a single resolution: the condemnation of Stevens and the hands-off policy of noninterference.

The Morgan Report

In the Senate, where the Democrats had only a slight majority, the Foreign Relations Committee, chaired by pro-annexation Senator John Morgan (D-Alabama), held hearings on the overthrow. Back in 1887, Morgan had sponsored the secret Senate amendment which ceded Pearl Harbor to the United States in the Reciprocity Treaty.

Morgan failed to convince Committee members to agree with his opinions, so he issued a report in February, 1894 approving Stevens' actions and urged recognition of the Provisional Government.

Nearly all of Morgan's witnesses supported annexation, so it is not surprising that Senator Morgan's report vindicated everyone involved in the Hawaiian affair, except the Queen and her Cabinet.

Former U.S. Minister John Stevens told the Senate panel that he had been in Hawai'i just one year when: "I came to the conclusion that the annexation of those islands was inevitable, or something else."[59] Furthermore, Stevens accused Queen Lili'uokalani of "exercising dictatorial powers" and of being "semibarbaric" and "maddened".[60]

The Morgan report concluded that U.S. relations with Hawai'i were unique, and should not be judged by the normal rules of conduct between nations.

However, Senator Morgan didn't condone establishing a U.S.

protectorate over Hawai'i. The remaining eight members of the Senate Foreign Relations Committee, four Democrats and four Republicans, approved those parts of the report which followed the positions of their respective political parties.

U.S. Senator Morgan revealed his annexation bias with this declaration:

> ...Hawai'i is an American state, and is embraced in the American commercial and military system. This fact has been frequently and firmly stated by our government...The United States will not admit the right of any foreign government to acquire any interest or control in the Hawaiian Islands that is in any way prejudicial or even threatening toward the interest of the United States or her people...

Senator Morgan further complained that the people of Hawai'i were subordinate "to the divine right of a monarchy, whose title to such divinity originated in the most slavish conditions of pagan barbarity."[61]

Both the Blount and Morgan Reports agreed on the basic facts of what happened in January, 1893, but offered different conclusions.

Blount concluded that the behavior and actions of Stevens, the presence and purpose of U.S. soldiers on shore, and the hasty recognition of the Provisional Government were legally and morally wrong.

In contrast, Senator Morgan concluded that Stevens' and Wiltse's actions were both legally and morally right. The Morgan Report did not dispute the intent to overthrow the Kingdom or to annex Hawai'i to America.

The Morgan Report charged that Minister Stevens and Commander Wiltse demonstrated "the privilege of interference", allowing them to rightfully take virtually any diplomatic or military action. Senator Morgan said Hawai'i was a special case. The United States has "always exerted the privilege of interference" in Hawaii's domestic affairs, which "...would not be justified, under our view of the international law" if the same actions were taken in Canada, Cuba, or Mexico.[62]

Senator Morgan added:

> ...The attitude of the United States toward Hawai'i was in moral effect that of a friendly protectorate. It has been a settled policy of the United States that if it should turn out that Hawai'i, for any cause, should not be able to maintain an independent government, that country would be encouraged in its tendency to gravitate toward political union with this country. [63]

Senator Morgan chose to ignore Hawaii's sovereign independence by approving American violation of international protocol and approving the landing of armed troops. He condoned the military action if it was done to protect U.S. citizens in another country. Senator Morgan contended:

> ...It seems that neither Minister Stevens nor Capt. Wiltse, then fully comprehended the fact that the United States had the right, of its own authority, to send the troops on shore for the purpose of supplying to American citizens resident there the protection of law...[64]

Senator Morgan concluded that American diplomats in Hawai'i:

> ...have the right to much larger liberty of action in respect to the internal affairs of (Hawai'i) than would be the case with any other country with which we have no peculiar or special relations. [65]

Would that "larger liberty of action" have included acts of war by the United States against the Hawaiian Kingdom?

Senator Morgan avoided that question. When he said: "By "landing troops in Honolulu there may have been an invasion," he tried to make a thin distinction between invasion and an act of war. He explained:

> ...If the Queen, or the people, or both acting in conjunction, had opposed the landing of the troops from the *Boston* with armed resistance, their invasion would have been an act of war. But when their landing was not opposed by any objection, protest, or resistance the state of war did not supervene, and there was no irregularity or want of authority to place the troops on shore.[66]

In other words, Senator Morgan reasoned that the American invasion was not an act of war because no resistance or counter-force was offered. Had the Queen resisted the United States military forces, then the landing of American troops would have been considered an act of war. The Queen sought to avoid bloodshed, so she acquiesced to an invasion that was not truly an invasion because America had the right to take hostile action against the Hawai'i monarchy.

Morgan's Report reveals how far America could go to violate international law, and then approve the wrong-doing after the fact.

Considering the tone of the Morgan Committee Report and the expansion-minded Senate, U.S. Senator David Turpie (D-Indiana), introduced a resolution encouraging Hawai'i to establish and maintain its own form of government, without interference from the United States. The Senate approved the resolution by unanimous vote, 55 to 0, with 30 abstentions on May 31, 1894.[67]

Thus, both houses of Congress passed different resolutions, giving the President a signal to establish a "hands-off policy".

Should President Cleveland be remembered as an honest and courageous President who criticized the sins of U.S. Minister Stevens and Captain Wiltse and apologized to the Queen? Or should he be remembered for refusing to call out the soldiers to undo what he admitted were wrongful acts?

View from Kawaiaha'o Church to Diamond Head (1895)

Historian Allan Nevins wrote that President Cleveland deserves praise:

> ...(I)n an era of international land-grabbing, Cleveland, despite angry sneers, had insisted that the United States should meet the loftiest obligations of honesty and unselfishness; in an era when the rights of small nations were almost universally trampled on, he had displayed a sensitive consideration for one of the weakest of them all. [68]

Queen Lili'uokalani is Arrested

By late 1893, Lorrin Thurston accepted the reality that the Provisional Government would have to wait four years or more until a friendlier American President would support annexation. Recognizing the long term needs of his government, Thurston wrote to Dole on November 19, 1893:

Republic of Hawai'i soldiers looking for escaped members of the Wilcox Revolt in Mānoa (1895)

I believe the time has fully arrived for a change to a permanent form of government, on the lines previously indicated. I favor not less than five years for a readjustment and settling down period, before elections take place. There is much in a name. Call it 'The Republic of Hawai'i.' It will not be a full exponent of the republican principle but that is the central thought around which it is gathered and into which it will develop in time.[69]

The Provisional Government never intended to be a democracy.

The Government arrested outspoken native newspaper editors for libel, passed a law regulating newspaper printing, kept suspects in jail without bail, and deported some American and British citizens.

U.S. Minister Willis reported to Gresham:

**Republic of Hawai'i soldiers blockade
'Iolani Palace during the 1895 Wilcox Revolt**

It is impossible to exaggerate the unhappy condition of this people, nor can I, in words...Almost every
movement is under espionage, the most meaningless
expression is given important significance, and
speeches are quoted which were never delivered or
thought of.[70]

Native Hawaiians and Asians were denied the right to vote
because they would win elections and control the government,
based on the size of their population. The Provisional Government would have none of that. It was a government of, by, and for
the Caucasians.

These biases were substantiated by a statement of Charles L.
Carter, a member of the Provisional Government's Annexation
Committee. He told the *New York World* newspaper:

There is such a large number of Chinese and other

cheap laborers on the islands who cannot be trusted to vote intelligently that if universal suffrage was declared the whites who represent almost the entire business interest of the country, would be outvoted and powerless.[71]

Admiral Joseph Skerrett reported to the Secretary of Navy on June 28, 1893 that the Provisional Government was "not elected by the vote of the people and it is believed, were it submitted to a popular vote, the present Government would be ousted."

Skerrett added: "It would appear that the iron heel of military law is really what serves to keep the Provisional Government in authority."[72]

As long as Grover Cleveland was President, the Provisional Government knew annexation would remain a stalemate. In a public relations gesture, the Provisional Government chose an historic American day – July 4, 1894, to adopt and proclaim the constitution of the new independent Republic of Hawai'i.

There was minimal participation by native Hawaiians after the Republic was established. Many native Hawaiians refused to take a loyalty oath to support the new government.

The new Constitution established strict voting qualifications, so few native Hawaiians or Asians could qualify as voters, even if they had wanted to. As a result, the voter decline was substantial.

For example, in 1890, native Hawaiians accounted for about 75% of the 13,593 registered voters. There were 11,671 votes for the House of Representatives, and only 3,187 votes for the House of Nobles. Due to the income and property restrictions of the Bayonet Constitution, few native Hawaiians qualified to vote for the Nobles. By 1894, a total of only 4,477 people registered to vote – a 67% decline.[73]

When an ill-fated revolt to restore the monarchy failed on January 16, 1895, most of the people arrested were native Hawaiians, including Prince Kūhiō and his brother Prince Kawānanakoa, and Queen Lili'uokalani.

Rifles and bombs were found buried in the Queen's garden.

The nervous Provisional Government charged Queen Lili'uokalani with treason. She was convicted, and sentenced to five years imprisonment.

Her sentence was reduced to eight months of house arrest in 'Iolani Palace from January to September, 1895, followed by five months under "house arrest" at Washington Place until February, 1896, followed by eight months of confinement to O'ahu – a total sentence of nearly two years.[74]

Prince Jonah Kūhiō

Others, including Robert Wilcox, who were arrested for plotting to overthrow the Provisional Government received death sentence penalties, which were eventually reduced to lengthy prison sentences. The Provisional Government, concerned about its public image in the United States, deliberately waited – at the request of Attorney General William O. Smith – before commuting the death sentences, so as to appear humane.[75]

The Provisional Government tricked Queen Lili'uokalani into formally abdicating her throne. Prior to her January 24 trial, the Provisional Government encouraged royalists to tell the Queen that she could save her supporters from the death penalty by giving up all rights to the throne. Neither the Queen nor her followers knew that the Provisional Government had decided, two weeks earlier, to commute all the death sentences.

After receiving full Hawai'i Republic citizenship in 1897, Lili'uokalani traveled to Washington, D.C. to oppose annexation.

Annexation

"We learn fast in war time.... "
—U.S. Congressman Robert Hitt (R-Illinois)

"As I look back upon the first steps in this miserable business, and as I contemplate the means used to complete the outrage, I am ashamed of the whole affair."
—former President Grover Cleveland

Japanese Immigration Crisis

By 1897, Hawai'i sugar planters had invited 25,000 Japanese to work as cheap contract laborers. This amounted to nearly one-fourth of the total population in Hawai'i and most of the plantation labor force.

Concerned about the excessive Japanese population, the Republic of Hawai'i passed laws allowing entrance only to Japanese immigrants who were "free laborers" possessing $50 in their pockets.

Japan protested when more than 1,000 Japanese "free laborers" were denied admittance, and accused of trying to enter Hawai'i illegally. In May, Japan sent two warships to seek restitution for those denied entrance, and to protect the rights of its citizens. Not surprisingly, the Republic of Hawai'i asked America's new President William McKinley, a Republican annexationist, for help. McKinley was inaugurated two months earlier, in March, 1897.

At the same time, Japan objected to the proposed 1897 annexation of Hawai'i to the United States, since it might endanger the rights of Japanese citizens in Hawai'i. Tension increased, but war with Japan was considered unlikely.

Annexation, Japan complained, was detrimental to its

Asian plantation workers cutting sugar cane

nationals. President McKinley expressed concern that Japan might try to annex Hawai'i before the United States could.

President McKinley told U.S. Senator George Hoar (R-Massachusetts):

> We cannot let the islands go to Japan...Japan has her eye on them. Her people are crowding in there. I am satisfied they do not go there voluntarily, as ordinary immigrants, but that Japan is pressing them in there, in order to get possession before anybody can interfere.[1]

American politicians and newspapers "attacked" the Japanese with a war of words and a barrage of racial stereotypes. After a year of negotiation, the Hawaiian Government settled the immigration dispute by paying Japan $75,000 in July, 1898 – clearing the way for American annexation.[2]

President McKinley Supports Annexation

The Americans who controlled the Provisional Government and Republic of Hawai'i knew what they wanted: annexation.

For four years, the Caucasian leaders of Hawaii's Government patiently made repeated overtures for annexation to the United States. Finally, in 1897, they gained a friend in the White House when Ohio Governor and former U.S. Senator William McKinley, the author of the despised McKinley Tariff Law, succeeded Grover Cleveland as President.

President William McKinley

McKinley campaigned on an annexation platform that stated: "The Hawaiian Islands should be controlled by the United States and no foreign power should be permitted to interfere with them."

The Republican Party's manifest destiny platform also supported a free Cuba, a canal across Central America linking the Atlantic and Pacific Oceans, and purchasing the Danish West Indies (now called the U.S. Virgin Islands).

Excited with opportunity, the Republic of Hawai'i quickly sent a new commission to Washington D.C. to negotiate a treaty. The new administration welcomed the Hawai'i delegation.

The Annexation Treaty was signed on June 16, 1897, three months after McKinley's inauguration. President Dole called a special session of the Republic Senate to ratify the document.

On September 7, native Hawaiians submitted petitions and

resolutions protesting annexation to Hawai'i Republic President Sanford Dole and to the U.S. Congress. The native Hawaiian petitions asked that annexation be decided by a public vote.

Again, the wishes of the native Hawaiians were ignored. Two days later, the Hawai'i Senate voted unanimously to ratify the Annexation Treaty on September 9, 1897. Voters in Hawai'i were not permitted to ratify the Annexation Treaty.

Now it was up to the U.S. Senate.

Annexation Arguments in the U.S.

Annexation debates in the U.S. Senate pointed to the same historical, constitutional, and moral issues in 1897 as in 1893.

Historical Concerns

The acquisition of Hawai'i was considered:

- inconsistent with traditional foreign policy precedents against "entangling alliances" and against policies that encouraged imperialism; and

- contrary to America's 50-year old policy of supporting Hawaii's independence, based on the 1842 "Tyler Doctrine"

Constitutional and Legal Concerns

- the native Hawaiians never consented to the temporary Provisional Government, and strongly opposed annexation. Without a popular vote, annexation was like accepting "stolen property."[3]

- the Provisional Government had no right to cede Hawai'i to the United States

- President Cleveland, in his 1893 message to Congress, had called American participation in the overthrow an illegal act of war

- the overthrow violated international law and several U.S.-Hawai'i treaties

Racial Concerns

Public opinion on racial lines ran rampant: On the one hand, there were bitter denunciations about the inferiority of Hawaii's native and Asian populations, while on the other hand, there was genuine concern for the self-governing rights of native Hawaiians.

Senator David Turpie (D-Indiana), a leader of the anti-annexation movement, said:

> There is a native population in the islands of about 40,000. They are not illiterate; they are not ignorant. A very large majority can read and write both languages, English and Hawaiian, and they take a very lively and intelligent interest in the affairs of their own country...Any treaty which had been made without consulting (native Hawaiians) should be withdrawn and ought never to have been sanctioned.[4]

Four years earlier, James Blount noted that an 1890 census revealed that more than 67% of the native Hawaiians could read and write. In contrast, about 90% of the Chinese and Japanese and 75% of the Portuguese were illiterate.[5]

Other Concerns

Several interest groups waged a vigorous campaign against annexation:

- mainland sugar interests feared competition from imported Hawaiian sugar

- organized labor opposed Hawaii's unique contract labor system, and

- political groups such as the prominent Anti-Imperialist League, opposed American expansion. Prominent Anti-Imperialist League members included former President Grover Cleveland, William Jennings Bryan, labor leader Samuel Gompers, industrialist Andrew Carnegie, Harvard University President Charles Eliot, philosopher William James, social worker Jane Addams, and author Mark Twain.[6]

Many in the U.S. criticized Hawaii's contract labor system, calling it similar to slavery.[7] Four of Hawaii's eight largest sugar planters opposed annexation because they worried about finding cheaply-paid workers.[8]

However the most effective argument against the 1897 Annexation Treaty urged the United States not to establish an imperialistic policy of expansion in the Pacific.

President McKinley knew it would be difficult for the Senate to ratify the treaty, so he considered a novel approach. During a March 15, 1897 meeting with Senate President William Frye (R-Maine) and former Secretary of State John Foster — before treaty negotiations were finalized with Hawai'i — the President admitted that annexation lacked the necessary two-thirds support in the Senate, and he suggested a joint resolution, which required a mere simple majority vote in each house.

The joint resolution option was seriously discussed throughout 1897, but President McKinley tried the traditional annexation treaty approach. He submitted a treaty to the Senate on June 16. The U.S. Senate took no action until December. After much debate and many delays, the chances of getting a two-thirds vote appeared slim.

Annexation easily held a majority support of the full Senate, but it fell a few votes shy of achieving the required two-thirds vote. As a result, the annexation treaty stalled in 1897.

On December 6, 1897, F.M. Hatch, the Hawai'i Minister to the U.S. said if the treaty failed, "The fight will go on by joint resolution or bill."[9] A month later, in January, 1898, Sanford Dole said that McKinley told him the joint resolution would be used if the Senate didn't pass the annexation treaty.[10]

Annexationists such as Assistant Navy Secretary Theodore Roosevelt, prominent naval historian Captain Alfred Thayer Mahan, and Senator Henry Cabot Lodge (R-Massachusetts) did their best to persuade fence-sitting Senators to support annexation. Not all Democrats were anti-imperialists. Several joined with Republicans to support annexation.

Annexation and War Hysteria

Fate intervened as the United States tangled with Spain over Cuba and the Philippines.

President McKinley, in his inauguration address declared emphatically: "We want no wars of conquest,"[11] but he yielded to strong public opinion. The American people wanted war.

People believed the Frederic Remington cartoons published in the widely-circulated national Hearst newspapers about wretched conditions in Cuba. The cartoon impressions were the inventions of an imaginative artist, sketching political pictures under orders from his publisher. It didn't matter that many of the cartoons were lies.

Then tragedy struck an opportunity for the annexation cause. The battleship, *U.S.S. Maine* blew up under mysterious circumstances on February 15, 1898, in Havana Harbor, killing 260 people. A month later, President McKinley sent Spain an ultimatum to get out of Cuba, or else.

Two months later, Spain agreed to virtually all of President McKinley's demands, but it didn't matter. Congress voted to declare war with Spain on April 20.

U.S. Army Camp McKinley near Diamond Head during the Spanish-American War (1898)

The Spanish-American war was one of the briefest in American history. The United States gained victory in three months. President McKinley dictated peace conditions on July 30, and Spain signed a preliminary peace treaty on August 12.

To the McKinley Administration, the possibility of not achieving Hawaiian annexation during wartime hysteria generated creative thinking and fast action about the legislative process, which led to the joint resolution. The lack of a precedent would be overlooked.

During wartime, politicians and people are more inclined to rally around the flag for anything they believe is patriotic and necessary to ensure military victory.

By whatever legislative means necessary, Congress voted to annex Hawai'i while the brief war was still in progress. Annexation was caught-up in wartime hysteria and war-time expediency since the United States felt it must have a mid-Pacific American base to support its military effort.

Why was Hawai'i so important?

Not surprisingly, the two most important reasons given by U.S. Senate and House annexation reports were based on Hawaii's strategic global location. The United States was concerned with:

- preventing another nation from gaining a military base in the North Pacific, and protecting America's West Coast

- obtaining the commercial trade of the islands

Expediency, however, was a more important consideration. The House Report on annexation stated:

> ...United States must act NOW to preserve the results of its past policy, and to prevent the dominance in Hawai'i of a foreign people...It is no longer a question of whether Hawai'i shall be controlled by the native Hawaiian or by some foreign people; but the question is, What foreign people shall control Hawai'i?[12]

During the war, America's naval warships needed a coaling station for fuel to transport soldiers and supplies to the Philippines to fight the Spanish. Admiral George Dewey's victory against Spain at Manila could not be weakened by lack of supplies. Anything less than the annexation of Hawai'i, some argued, would keep Hawai'i neutral.

Congressman Robert Hitt (R-Illinois) declared:

> For a war of defense the Hawaiian Islands are...most essential...Until they were lately awakened by the war and the movement to re-enforce Admiral Dewey, (people) have not thought much about the exposed situation of our western coast in case of war with a really great power or the necessity of possessing these islands confronting our Pacific Coast.
>
> We learn fast in war time.... [13]

Annexation debate in the U. S. Senate was conducted behind closed doors in a secret session on May 31, 1898. Senator Justin Morrill (R-Vermont) charged:

> Here the Senate was informed about it (the secret session) after the Secretary (of State) had signed the treaty, but even the Senate did not permit itself to discuss it except in secret session until its paucity of votes was disclosed; and it came originally in the form of a treaty.... [14]

Some Senators attending the secret session questioned the secrecy of anything discussed there.

However annexation proponents insisted on the secret session not because of concern for war security, but because they feared political embarrassment if the annexation measure were defeated. They used the war with Spain as an opportunity to provide "the heat that generated annexation," as Senator John Morgan described it.[15]

Congressman De Alva Alexander (R-New York) explained on June 11: "The annexation of the Hawaiian Islands, for the first time in our history, is presented to us as a war necessity."[16]

This idea was echoed by other Congressmen such as Representative Richmond Pearson (R-North Carolina) who said: "I believe that this is a necessary step in the successful prosecution of the war with Spain." [17] Congressman William Mesick (R-Michigan), who converted to the annexation side after the battle of Manila Bay, announced: "it now becomes our manifest duty to possess the Hawaiian Islands." [18]

Pearl Harbor as a Military Necessity

The need to use Hawai'i as a strategic naval and commercial base for refueling and re-supply had long been recognized. The popular war historian and scholar, U.S. Navy Captain Alfred Thayer Mahan, convinced a generation of American policy makers that America needed a strong navy to become a world power.

Mahan's influence and America's new manifest destiny philosophy surged the United States Navy from the world's 12th largest in 1880 to the third largest by 1900.

Widespread recognition of Hawaii's significance increased with military victories in the Philippines. After Admiral Dewey's victory in Manila on May 1, American expansionists insisted that the United States must annex Hawai'i to safely send supplies and reinforcements to American troops in the Philippines.

Although the United States had obtained Pearl Harbor a decade earlier in 1887, nothing had been done to develop the site as a naval base. America's rights to Pearl Harbor derived from a treaty that could be terminated by a new treaty. Pearl Harbor now became a primary objective of annexation.

Annexationists argued that America must have permanent rights to Pearl Harbor, and only annexation could provide it. At the beginning of the Spanish-American War, Honolulu was the only coaling station available to the United States in the Pacific, except for Samoa, whose geographic location in the South Pacific was less important.

Victory at Manila Bay provided the thrust that gave Hawai'i to the annexationists. Three days later, on May 4, Congressman Francis Newlands (D-Nevada) introduced an annexation resolution in the U.S. House of Representatives.

Why a Joint Resolution, Not a Treaty?

After many failed treaty attempts, annexation was finally accomplished in 1898 through a Joint Congressional Resolution.

What's the difference? A joint resolution requires only a majority vote of the U.S. House and Senate, while a treaty needs a two-thirds vote of the Senate.

It is usually difficult enough to get half the members of Congress to agree on any major legislation, but attaining a two-thirds vote is even more difficult. Just a few Senators, namely one-third plus one, can deny the wishes of an extraordinary majority.

The annexation treaty had majority support in the Senate, but it was a few votes shy of attaining two-thirds support.

President McKinley finally yielded to expedience, and supported a simple resolution.

Congressman Edgar Crumpacker (R-Indiana), an opponent of annexation, candidly told House colleagues on June 14, 1898: "...the treaty required the assent of two-thirds of the Senators, and it became apparent that it could not command that assent, so it has been abandoned and this expedient invented...."[19]

Congressman Jonathan Dolliver (R-Iowa), an annexation supporter, told the House:

> Now for the second time a treaty has been negotiated annexing these islands, and the opposition of less than a majority in the Senate has held up the treaty, and we are driven to the unusual expedient of a joint resolution of Congress to accomplish a thing which ought to have been accomplished nearly ten years ago. [20]

Despite vocal opposition, the U.S. House approved the Newlands Resolution, 209 to 91, six weeks later on June 15.

On June 30, U.S. Senator William Bate (D-Tennessee) condemned the curious resolution approach, calling it:

> ...an innovation upon all precedents known in the history of this country and its legislation that we should have a resolution from the House of Representatives before the Senate involving the precise question that is still pending in the nature of a treaty. [21]

The U.S. Senate defeated amendments to abolish contract labor, and to require all adult Hawaiians to approve annexation by a vote. Then, after a three-week long filibuster by Senate oppo-

**Lowering the Hawaiian Flag from 'Iolani Palace
during Annexation Ceremony, August 12, 1898**

nents, the U.S. Senate passed the Newlands Resolution, 42 to 21, with 26 abstentions on July 6.[22]

Ironically, the Senate gave the resolution a two-thirds vote. Since the resolution needed a simple majority vote, its passage was considered a forgone conclusion during war time, so the "fence-sitters" in Congress voted for it too. Wasting no time, President McKinley signed the annexation resolution a day later, July 7.

The next day, former President Grover Cleveland sadly remarked in a letter to Richard Olney, who had served as his Attorney General and Secretary of State:

> Hawai'i is ours. As I look back upon the first steps in this miserable business, and as I contemplate the means used to complete the outrage, I am ashamed of the whole affair. [23]

July 14, 1898

(story about the Spanish-American War in the right column)

Formal transfer of sovereignty occurred on August 12, 1898. Hawai'i officially became a Territory of the United States.

Here's what war hysteria accomplished: seven months after annexing Hawai'i, the U.S. acquired Guam, the Philippines, Puerto Rico, Wake Island, and Guantánamo Bay as a naval base in Cuba. In addition, Spain paid the United States $20 million.

America would have acquired all of Cuba, but an amendment from Senator Henry Teller (R-Colorado) to the declaration of war against Spain disclaimed annexation.

The United States, with its powerful navy, emerged from the Spanish-American War as a world power with global possessions.

Was Annexation Legal?

"...The proposed annexation of the Hawaiian Islands constitutes a new departure in the policy of our Government...."
— U.S. Congressman James Mann (R-Illinois)

Hawai'i and Texas Compared

Was the American annexation of Hawai'i legal?

Back in 1893, anti-expansionists questioned the constitutionality of annexing Hawai'i by treaty. Now in 1898, the critics questioned the constitutionality of using a joint resolution.

The main argument against the joint resolution approach was that the United States could gain territory only via its constitutional treaty-making powers. To acquire Hawai'i by a joint resolution would bypass the President's and Senate's authority, and set a dangerous precedent.

Annexation supporters pointed to the acquisition of Texas in 1845 by joint resolution as a precedent. Critics said Texas was brought into the Union legally under Congress' power to admit new states.

Hawai'i was being acquired as a territory, not a state, so anti-annexationists said the Texas acquisition was not a legitimate precedent. The annexation of Texas was later ratified by a popular vote. No popular vote was mandated for Hawai'i.

An effort was made in the U.S. Senate to require a popular vote in Hawai'i by all adult males, but it was defeated 20-42, with 27 abstentions, prior to the eventful vote for annexation.

Until Hawaii's annexation in 1898, all populated U.S. territories except for Texas had been annexed by treaty.

Both Texas and Hawai'i were independent foreign nations that became United States territories via joint resolutions.

Sanford Dole receives the Annexation Resolution from U.S. Minister Harold Sewall, on August 12, 1898.

Texas won its independence from Mexico in 1836 and negotiated a treaty with the United States for annexation in 1844. The United States Senate rejected this treaty by nearly a two-thirds vote against annexation. In protest, Texas considered a treaty of alliance with Great Britain or France. This angered the American people, and despite the controversy of admitting Texas as a slave state, Congress quickly passed a joint resolution in 1845 admitting the Texas Republic as the 28th state.

A joint congressional resolution left it up to the President to accept Texas by three methods: treaty; by agreement with Texas under legislative act; or by a convention chosen by the people of Texas.[1] Texas preferred holding a convention, and the people of Texas voted for annexation.

In two important ways, the Texas and Hawai'i annexations were similar:

- Many expatriate American citizens lived in Texas and Hawai'i when annexation was considered in each respective Republic.

- In each Republic, annexation by a joint resolution was achieved only after the U.S. Senate failed to ratify a treaty.

The U.S. Senate Report on Hawaiian annexation stated that the joint resolution for annexing Texas "clearly establishes the precedent that Congress has the power to annex a foreign state...upon the consent of such foreign government obtained in any authentic way."[2]

Those who opposed annexation argued against the precedent. If Texas could be annexed as a state by Congressional resolution, then why couldn't Hawai'i be annexed as a territory?

Congressman James Mann (R-Illinois) addressed that question when he told Congress:

> It is not necessary to deny that the proposed annexation of the Hawaiian Islands constitutes a new departure in the policy of our Government, for whether it does or not makes no difference...The Republican Party...has never shrunk from doing that which is right and advantageous because it might be called a new departure.[3]

Nor did it matter to President McKinley if the resolution had no clear precedent. The influential U.S. Senator Henry Cabot Lodge (R-Massachusetts), a close friend of the President said: "The President has been very firm about it and means to annex the Islands anyway...."[4]

President McKinley raised an old theme when he told his personal secretary George Cortelyou: "We need Hawai'i just as much and a good deal more than we did California. It is manifest destiny."[5]

President McKinley sent Congress this message with the

Annexation Treaty on June 16, 1897: "Despite successive denials and postponements (annexation) has been merely a question of time. Annexation is not a change, it is a consummation."[6]

Politicians sometimes do what they believe is right. Sometimes they do what they think is best. Hopefully, what they do is both right and for the best. During wartime hysteria, there tends to be less reliance on precedent, and more reliance on expediency.

No Public Vote in Hawai'i

How could the United States annex a foreign population without assurance that a majority of the people wanted it?

Congress knew that most native Hawaiians were disenfranchised, and therefore, without representation in the legislative and executive levels of government. Congress also knew that the Queen was overthrown by American involvement.

There was one important difference in the annexations of Texas and Hawai'i: in Texas, the people were allowed to vote on annexation. No popular vote was taken in Hawai'i. This sensitive issue wasn't settled until a vote for statehood was finally taken in 1940 – more than 40 years after annexation.

Opponents of Hawaiian annexation claimed that the Texas plebiscite set a precedent for requiring a popular vote on annexation in Hawai'i. Annexation proponents argued that the Texas Legislature didn't mandate that a popular vote must approve annexation. The plebiscite was allowed at the discretion of the President of the Texas Republic. The annexation of Texas was completed in July, 1845 when the Texas constitutional convention ratified the resolution – prior to the October plebiscite.

What would have happened if the Texas voters rejected annexation?

Did Any Native Hawaiians Support Annexation?

The historical record, based on a statement by Republic of

Hawai'i Attorney General William O. Smith, reveals that no more than six native Hawaiians were present in the Hawai'i Legislature when the 1894 Constitution of Hawai'i was adopted. The Constitution called for Hawaii's annexation.

President Dole offered these reasons for annexation:

- a growing menace to the population by immigration

- the threat of great naval powers

- need for United States' development of resources, and

- it was in the best interests of all the people of Hawai'i

Native Hawaiians submitted petitions and protests to the Hawai'i Legislature, President Dole, the U.S. Congress, and President McKinley, but to no avail.

The resolution that ratified the 1897 Annexation Treaty was adopted unanimously by the Hawai'i Senate the same day, September 9, 1897.

A native Hawaiian, Senator J. Kauhane, serving as Vice President of the Republic Senate, voted for annexation. He was the only Senator who seemed to be a native Hawaiian by virtue of a Hawaiian last name.

About 29,000 native Hawaiians submitted to Congress a "monster petition" of 1897, protesting American annexation.

J. Kauhane

A Congressional investigation of this petition alleged that many names on it were fraudulent. Nevertheless, many of the 29,000 names were allowed to remain, representing the vast majority of the 31,000 "native Hawaiians" living in the Islands. This population figure may be compared with the 3,196 actual voters in the first election under the 1894 Republic of Hawai'i Constitution held in 1896, and the 2,687 voters for Representatives in 1897.

U.S. Congressmen agreed that most, if not all, native Hawaiians opposed annexation. Senator Donelson Caffery (D-Louisiana) told the Senate on June 28, 1898, that "the people of Hawai'i do not want annexation...When I speak of the people of Hawai'i, I speak of the native Hawaiians."[7]

As stated earlier, most Hawaiians were disenfranchised by the Republic. However, after Hawai'i became a U.S. territory in 1898, the native Hawaiians did their best to get even. All Hawaiians who passed a literacy test were allowed to vote, so by sheer numbers, they dominated the Territorial Legislature. (The Governor was appointed by the U.S. President).

Voters sent Robert Wilcox, the leader of native Hawaiian insurrections in 1889 and 1895, as their first delegate to the U.S. Congress. Hawaii's first Territorial Legislature, in 1901 was dominated by native Hawaiians and Home Rule advocates who protested annexation by delaying bills, failing to pass the appropriation bill, and calling for Governor Dole's removal due to incompetence.

Hawai'i Statehood Compared to Other States

Hawai'i was finally admitted to statehood in 1959 after waiting more than 60 years as a territory.

Texas and Hawai'i, which were both annexed by joint resolutions rather than treaties, are the only two exceptions to the constitutional requirement that new territory may be acquired by treaties with foreign nations.

Thirty-four states had established territorial governments and served waiting periods before seeking admission as states. Three states – Texas, Florida and California – were admitted directly as states.

Only five states experienced lengthy territorial periods before gaining statehood: Utah, 46 years; Arizona, 49 years; Hawai'i, 61 years; New Mexico, 62 years; and Alaska, 92 years.

History of Hawai'i Statehood

Two years after annexation, Hawai'i established a Territorial Government. Three years later, in 1903, the Hawai'i Territorial Legislature petitioned Congress for statehood.

The political desire for statehood was best summarized in 1959 by John Burns, Hawaii's Delegate to Congress (and future Governor), in an article for the Congressional Record, "Statehood and Hawaii's people."[8]

Burns acknowledged that the Hawaiian people distrusted the Provisional Government, whose rule was more restrictive than the monarchy had been. Many people were prevented from voting, while power remained in the hands of the propertied class. Burns said annexation was unpopular based on resentment against the particular ruling party, not due to animosity toward the United States.

According to Burns, two Hawai'i members of a commission that wrote the document establishing the Territorial Government – Governor Sanford Dole and Hawai'i Supreme Court Justice (and future Governor) Walter Frear – wanted to impose property and income requirements for voting. Such a provision would have denied most native Hawaiians from voting. Only the "adamant insistence" of U.S. Senator Benjamin Tillman (D-South Carolina) succeeded in blocking the restrictive measures.

The Hawai'i Territorial Governor, however, continued his restrictive policies. The Territorial Legislature passed measures for creating county governments, while the Territorial Governor

50th State, not 49th –
Pualani Avon (l) and
Congressional Delegate
Joseph Farrington
(r) promoted this
Statehood video in
Washington, D.C.

repeatedly vetoed them. This produced a Congressional investigation. As a result, Congress called for the Territory to organize county governments quickly or Congress would do so. After this directive, the Territorial Governor allowed a local government bill to pass.

Many of the controlling economic and political Caucasian oligarchy opposed statehood for reasons of self-interest.

For 50 years, Caucasian elites ruled Hawai'i as a tightly-controlled, closed society. They controlled the political, economic, social and religious activities, especially at the plantation camps.

For example, Democratic Party candidates had to sneak into the plantations after dark. Plantation workers were carefully observed in the voting booth. If a voter dared to vote for the

Pearl Harbor with a view of Ford Island (1925)

Democratic ticket, the loop of a pencil hanging on a tight string directly over the Republican side of the ballot would move.[9]

By 1935, Hawai'i statehood was receiving broad-based support in Hawai'i. It was suggested that a plebiscite would determine if Hawai'i citizens wanted statehood. For the first time, in 1940, a plebiscite was held, and a majority of Hawaii's residents voted for statehood. Prospects for statehood, however, were delayed by World War II.

Numerous Congressional hearings on Hawai'i statehood confirmed that Hawai'i had met all the criteria for admission. Voters expressed their desire for statehood by approving, by a 3-to-2 margin, a proposed state constitution in the 1949 general election.

Now Congress procrastinated on ratifying Hawai'i statehood. Alaska and Hawai'i were both struggling for statehood when Hawai'i Congressional Delegate John Burns agreed to allow Alaska to be admitted first. The strategy worked. Congress finally approved Statehood for Hawai'i on March 12, 1959.

Bibliographical Notes

A Fragile Kingdom Seeks Respect

1. Ralph S. Kuykendall, The Hawaiian Kingdom, Volume I, 1778-1854, Foundation and Transformation, (Honolulu: University of Hawaii Press, 1968), p. 40-43. Hereafter cited as Kuykendall, vol. I.

2. Kuykendall, vol. I, p. 267.

3. Linda Menton and Eileen Tamura, A History of Hawai'i, (Honolulu: University of Hawai'i, 1989), p. 8.

4. Kuykendall, vol. I, p. 166.

5. Webster to Hawaiian delegation, December 19, 1842, U.S. Congress, House Executive Documents, 53 Congress 2nd Session, Washington, D.C. 1895, p. 44. Hereafter cited as Blount Report.

6. Tyler Doctrine, December 30, 1842, Blount Report, p. 39-40.

7. Kamehameha III to Paulet, February 25, 1843, Blount Report, p. 49.

8. Ibid., p. 50.

9. Kamehameha III proclamation, February 25, 1842, Blount Report, p. 51.

10. Kuykendall, vol. I, p. 215.

11. Native Hawaiians Study Commission: Report on the Culture, Needs and Concerns of Native Hawaiians, volume II, Honolulu, 1983 , p. 98. Hereafter cited as NHSC, vol. I or vol. II.

12. Instructions to Dillon, July, 1849, Kuykendall, vol. I, p. 391.

13. W.D. Alexander statement, July 18, 1893, Blount Report, p. 609.

14. Wyllie to Judd, Nov. 3, 1849, Kuykendall, vol. I, p. 384.

15. Kamehameha III proclamation, March 10, 1851, Blount Report, p. 88-89.

16. Ibid.

17. Kamehameha III to Pierce, March 31, 1851, Blount Report, p. 614.

18. Legislative resolution of June 21, 1851, Blount Report, p. 98.

19. Webster to Severance, July 14, 1851, Blount Report, p. 102.

20. Ibid.

21. Rives to Webster, July 22, 1851, Blount Report, p. 103-104.

22. Alexander statement, July 18, 1893, Blount Report, p. 608.

23. Kuykendall, vol. I, p. 409.

24. Ibid., p. 417.

25. Miller and Perrin to Kamehameha III, September 1, 1853, Kuykendall, vol. I, p. 417.

26. Marcy to Miller, November 20, 1853 in Kuykendall, vol. I, p. 418.

27. Marcy to Mason, December 16, 1853 in Blount Report, p. 106.

28. Marcy to Gregg, April 4, 1854, Blount Report, p. 121-122.

29. Kuykendall, vol. I, p. 421-426.

30. Proposed treaty, September 27, 1854, Blount Report, p. 622.

31. Wyllie to Lee, July 11, 1854, Blount Report, p. 625.

32. Marcy to Gregg, January 31, 1855, Ralph S. Kuykendall, The Hawaiian Kingdom, Volume II, 1854-1874, Twenty Critical Years, (Honolulu: University of Hawaii Press, 1966), p. 41. Hereafter cited as Kuykendall, vol. II.

33. Lee to Wyllie, July 14, 1855, Kuykendall, vol. II, p. 41.

34. Jacob Adler, The Journal of Prince Alexander Liholiho (Honolulu: University of Hawai'i Press, 1965), p. 108.

35. Kuykendall, vol. II, p. 38.

36. Gavan Daws, Shoal of Time: A History of the Hawaiian Islands, (New York: The MacMillan Company, 1968), p. 208.

37. McBryde to Seward, September 16, 1864, Blount Report, p. 137.

38. McCook to Seward, September 3, 1866, Blount Report, p. 139.

39. McCook to Seward, May 29, 1867, Sylvester K. Stevens, American Expansion in Hawaii, 1842-1898, (Harrisburg: Archives Publishing Co. of Pennsylvania, 1945), p. 99. Hereafter cited as Sylvester Stevens.

40. Seward to McCook, June 1867, Sylvester Stevens, p. 99.

41. Seward to McCook, September 12, 1867, Blount Report, p. 143.

42. Ibid.

43. Kuykendall, vol. II, p. 220.

44. Spalding to Spalding, April 14, 1869, Blount Report, p. 147.

45. Ibid.

46. Johnson, message to Congress, December 9, 1868, Blount Report, p. 146.

47. Ibid, p. 143.

48. Henry Peirce to Fish, February 25, 1871, Blount Report, p. 17.

49. Fish to President Pierce, March 25, 1873, Blount Report, p. 19.

50. *Polynesian,* January 26, 1850, Kuykendall, vol. I, p. 386.

51. Blount Report, p. 604.

52. Robert Schmitt, Demographic Statistics of Hawai'i (Honolulu: University of Hawai'i Press, 1968), p. 39.

53. McBryde to Seward, October 9, 1863, Blount Report, p. 135.

54. Henry Peirce to Fish, February 25, 1871, Blount Report, p. 17.

55. Stevens to Blaine March 20, 1890, Blount Report, p. 315-316.

56. Ibid., p. 316-317.

57. Peirce to Fish, February 17, 1873, Blount Report, p. 153.

58. Alexander and Schofield to Belknap, May 8, 1873, Blount Report, p. 154 and American Historical Review, Vol. 30, 1925, pp. 560-565.

59. Belknap to Alexander and Schofield, Kuykendall, vol. II, p. 248.

60. Blount Report, p. 158, and American Historical Review.

61. Henry Peirce to Fish, February 10, 1873, Blount Report, p. 153.

62. Information received from U.S. Army.

63. Blount Report, p. 646.

64. Henry Peirce to Fish, January 11, 1875, Sylvester Stevens, p. 124.

65. Sylvester Stevens, p. 125.

66. Ibid., p. 138.

67. Eugene Burns, The Last King of Paradise (New York: Pelligrini and Cudahy,

1952), p. 157. Hereafter cited as Burns.
  68. Peirce to Fish, February 3, 1876, Sylvester Stevens, p. 148.
  69. Lili'uokalani, Hawaii's Story by Hawaii's Queen (Rutland, Vermont: Charles E. Tuttle, Co., 1964), p. 55. Hereafter cited as Lili'uokalani.

European Imperialism and U.S. Manifest Destiny

  1. Claude Julien, America's Empire (New York: Pantheon Books, 1971), p. 52.
  2. Douglas L. Oliver, The Pacific Islands. Rev. Ed. (Cambridge: Harvard University Press, 1952).
  3. Kuykendall, vol. I, p. 386.
  4. Samuel Bemis, The American Secretaries of State and their Diplomacy, (New York: Pageant Book Company, 1958), p. 3-115.
  5. Ibid., p. 264-297.
  6. Blaine to Comly, December 1, 1881, Blount Report, p. 1157-1162.

Kalākaua: A Tragic King

  1. William Armstrong, Around the World with a King (Rutland, Vermont: Charles E. Tuttle, Co., 1977), p. 246. Hereafter cited as Armstrong.
  2. Lorrin A. Thurston, Memoirs of the Hawaiian Revolution. (Honolulu: Advertiser Publishing Co., Ltd., 1936), p. 21-22, 129. Hereafter cited as Thurston.
  3. Burns, p. 168.
  4. Burns, p. 176.
  5. Francis Conroy, The Japanese Frontier in Hawaii, 1868-1898, M.A. Thesis, (University of California, Kraus Reprint, Millwood, N.Y., 1980), p. 51-52. Hereafter cited as Conroy.
  6. Ralph S. Kuykendall, The Hawaiian Kingdom, Volume III, 1874-1893, The Kalakaua Dynasty, (Honolulu: University of Hawaii Press, 1968), p. 241. Hereafter cited as Kuykendall, vol. III.
  7. Armstrong, p. 199.
  8. Blaine to Comly, November 19, 1881, Blount Report, p. 1156.
  9. Armstrong, p. 58-59.
  10. Kathleen Dickenson Mellen, An Island Kingdom Passes (New York: Hastings House Publishers, 1958), p. 120.
  11. Armstrong, p. 198.
  12. Ibid., p. xxii.
  13. Jacob Adler, Claus Spreckels: The Sugar King in Hawaii, (Honolulu: University of Hawai'i Press, 1966), p. 100.
  14. Bayard to Merrill, January 8, 1887, Blount Report, p. 1165.
  15. Kuykendall, vol. III, p. 397.
  16. Sylvester Stevens, p. 181.
  17. Kuykendall, vol. III, p. 348.
  18. Thurston, p. 130.
  19. editorial, August 27, 1884, *Daily Bulletin,* Kuykendall, vol. III, p. 277.

20. Thurston, p. 137-138.
21. Ibid., p. 140.
22. Volney Ashford statement, Blount Report, p. 669.
23. Dole to Willis, December 23, 1893, Blount Report, p. 1281.
24. Kuykendall, vol. III, p. 348-9.
25. Sylvester Stevens, p. 152.
26. Merrill to Bayard, May 31, 1887, NHSC vol. I, p. 275.
27. Ibid., p. 275.
28. Ibid. p. 276.
29. Ibid., p. 275-276.
30. Kuykendall, III p. 364.
31. NHSC, vol. I, p. 277.
32. Ibid., p. 278.
33. Thurston, p. 64.
34. Ibid., p. 175.
35. Lili'uokalani, p. 181-182.
36. Kuykendall, vol. III, p. 371.
37. Bayard to Merrill, July 12, 1887, Blount Report, p. 1167.
38. Bayard to Merrill, September 30, 1887, Blount Report, p. 1168-9.
39. Blount Report, p. 594, 1136.
40. Thurston, p. 153.
41. A. Judd interview, May 16, 1893, Blount Report, p. 837.
42. Lili'uokalani p. 78.
43. Ibid., p. 177-178.
44. Ibid., p. 237-8.
45. Ibid., p. 178.
46. Kuykendall, vol. III, p. 401.
47. Merrill to Blaine, August 1, 1889, Blount Report, p. 179.
48. William Adam Russ, Jr., The Hawaiian Revolution 1893-1894, (Selinsgrove, Pennsylvania: Susquehanna University Press, 1959), p. 23. Hereafter cited as Russ, vol. I.
49. Ibid., p. 24.
50. Kimberly to Tracy, October 18, 1889, Blount Report, p. 1170.
51. Ibid.
52. Blaine to Tracy, November 6, 1889 and Tracy to Kimberly, November 13, 1889, Blount Report, 1171-1172.
53. Kuykendall, vol. III, p. 453.
54. Carol Thompson, John L. Stevens: A Study in the New Manifest Destiny. M.A. Thesis, Smith College, 1954, p. 7-18. Hereafter cited as Thompson.
55. Helena G. Allen, Betrayl of Lili'uokalani. (The Arthur H. Clark Company, Glendale, California, 1982), p. 218. Hereafter cited as Allen.
56. Lili'uokalani p. 243-4.
57. John L. Stevens and W.B. Oleson, Riches and Marvels of Hawaii, Philadelphia: Edgewood Publishing Company, 1900), p. 269.
58. Ibid, p. 267.

59. Ibid, p. 268.
60. Thompson, p. 5.
61. Alexander to Alexander, February 7, 1890, Kuykendall, vol. III, p. 452.
62. Stevens to Blaine, March 20, 1890, Blount Report, p. 315.
63. NHSC, vol. I, p. 292.
64. Kuykendall, vol. III, p. 461-462.
65. Ibid., p. 462.
66. Stevens to Blaine, August 19, 1890, Blount Report, p. 334.
67. Wodehouse to Foreign Office, August 29, 1890, Kuykendall, vol. III, p. 463.
68. Kalākaua to Synge, September 19, 1890, Kuykendall, vol. III, p. 463.
69. Kuykendall, vol. III, p. 464.
70. Ibid.

Radicals Seek Power

1. Stevens to Foster, November 20, 1892, Blount Report, p. 382.
2. Harrison to Blaine, October 14, 1891, Kuykendall, vol. III, p. 491.
3. Kuykendall, vol. III, p. 492, 499.
4. Ibid., p. 503.
5. Ibid., p. 504.
6. Ibid., p. 503.
7. Ibid., p. 519.
8. Ibid. p. 522.
9. Blaine to Harrison, August 10, 1891, Kuykendall, vol. III, p. 486
10. Stevens to Blaine, September 5, 1891, Blount Report, p. 350-351.
11. Stevens to Blaine, October 15, 1891, Kuykendall, vol. III, p. 502.
12. Stevens to Blaine, February 8, 1892, Blount Report, p. 353-354.
13. Stevens to Blaine, March 8, 1892, Blount Report, p.182.
14. Stevens to Blaine, on March 25, 1892, Russ, vol. I, p. 45
15. Stevens to Blaine April 2, 1892, Blount Report, p. 356-357.
16. Brown to Tracy, September 6, 1892, Blount Report, p. 183.
17. Stevens to Foster, November 20, 1892, Blount Report, p. 377-384.
18. Thurston, p. 229.
19. Ibid.
20. Ibid., p. 231.
21. Ibid., p. 232.
22. Thurston to Blaine, May 27, 1892, Julius Pratt, "The Hawaiian Revolution: A Re-Interpretation," Pacific Historical Review 1, No. 3, (1932), p. 289.
23. Ibid., p. 287.
24. Ibid., p. 274.
25. Ibid., p. 286.
26. The Nation, Vol. LVII, November 29, 1893, p. 381.
27. Wiltse to Tracy, October 12, 1892, Blount Report, p. 185.
28. Stevens to Foster, November 20, 1893, Blount Report, p. 380-381.
29. Hopkins to Thurston, November 15, 1892, Thurston, p. 234.

30. Thurston to Hopkins, December 14, 1892, Thurston, p. 239-240.
31. Thurston, p. 235.
32. Skerrett interview, April 8, 1893, Blount Report, p. 476.
33. Cornwell statement, April 24, 1893, Blount Report, p. 496.
34. Lili'uokalani, p. 230-31.
35. Ibid., p. 21.
36. Kuykendall, vol. III, p. 580-581.

Queen Llili'uokalani Yields to an American Conspiracy

1. Lucien Young, The Boston at Hawaii (Washington, D.C., 1898), p. 145.
2. Stevens statement, United States Senate Committee on Foreign Relations, Senate Report 227, 1894, volume I, p. 535. Hereafter cited as the Morgan Report.
3. Smith, Castle and Cooper statement, July 15, 1893, Blount Report, p. 955.
4. Lili'uokalani, p. 281.
5. Colburn and Cornwell statements, April 15 and 24, 1893, Blount Report, p. 498, 496.
6. Lili'uokalani, p. 385.
7. Smith, Castle and Cooper statement, Blount Report, p. 958.
8. Thurston, p. 247.
9. Kuykendall, vol. III, p. 587.
10. Thurston, p. 250.
11. Smith statement, Blount Report, p. 963.
12. Thurston to Foster, February 21, 1893, Kuykendall III, p. 588.
13. Smith statement, Blount Report, p. 963.
14. Wundenburg interview, May 15, 1893, Blount Report, p. 561.
15. Smith statement, Blount Report, p. 964.
16. Wundenburg interview, May 15, 1893, Blount Report, p. 1043.
17. Colburn and Parker statements, Blount Report, p. 499 and 905.
18. Blount Report, p. 501.
19. NHSC, v.2, p. 61.
20. Wundenburg statement, Blount Report, p. 492.
21. Stevens to Wiltse, January 16, 1893, Blount Report, p. 208.
22. Young, p. 186.
23. Young, p. 182.
24. NHSC, p. 296.
25. Skerrett statement, May 20, 1893, Blount Report, p. 538.
26. Cornwell statement, April 24, 1893, Blount Report, p. 495.
27. Stevens to Foster, NHSC, p. 63.
28. Wilson affidavit, May 9, 1893, Blount Report, p. 643.
29. Kuykendall, vol. III, p. 598.
30. Cleghorn to Stevens, January 16, 1893, Blount Report, p. 1058.
31. Kuykendall, vol. III, p. 367.
32. Russ, vol. I, p. 90.
33. Sanford B. Dole, Memoirs (Honolulu: Advertiser Publishing Co.), 1936, p.

78. Hereafter cited as Dole.

34. Thurston to Hopkins, December 14, 1893, Thurston, p. 239-240.

35. Trousseau statement, May 16, 1893, Blount Report, p. 991.

36. Queen's Ministers to Stevens, January 17, 1893, Blount Report, p, 529.

37. Damon statement, April 29, 1893, Blount Report, p. 506.

38. Dole, p. 86

39. Stevens statement, Morgan Report, vol. I, p. 547.

40. Stevens notice, January 17, 1893, Blount Report, p. 228.

41. Dole to Stevens, January 17, 1893, Blount Report, p. 565.

42. Lili'uokalani to Dole, January 17, 1893, Blount Report, p. 866.

43. Lili'uokalani, p. 354.

44. Lili'uokalani statement, Blount Report, p. 866.

45. Stevens to Foster, January 18, 1893, Blount Report, p. 208.

46. Lili'uokalani to Harrison, January 18, 1893, Blount Report, p. 219.

47. Lili'uokalani to Harrison, Blount Report, p. 867.

48. Lili'uokalani to Cleveland, January 31, 1893, Blount Report, p. 867-868.

49. Blount Report, p. 228-232.

50. Stevens to Wiltse, February 1, 1893, Blount Report, p. 404.

51. Kuykendall, vol. III, p. 608.

52. Stevens to Foster, February 1, 1893, Blount Report, p. 399-404.

53. Stevens to Foster, February 1, 1893, Blount Report, p. 401-404.

54. Foster to Stevens, February 11, 1893, Blount Report, p. 242.

55. Russ, vol. I, p. 113-115.

56. *New York Herald,* April 24, 1893, Thomas J. Osborne, Empire Can Wait (Kent State University Press, Kent, Ohio, 1981), p. 28. Hereafter cited as Osborne.

57. Harrison to Hines, February 3, 1893, Osborne, p. 9.

58. Thurston to Dole, February 9, 1893, Osborne, p. 139, ff5.

59. Foster to Harrison, February 16, 1893, Blount Report, p. 5.

60. Harrison Message, February 17, 1893, Blount Report, p. 197-198.

61. Stevens to Foster, March 1, 1893, Blount Report, p. 226.

62. Merze Tate, The United States and the Hawaiian Kingdom, (Westport, Connecticut: Greenwood Press, 1965), ff 2, p. 229.

63. Osborne, p. 11.

America's Dilemma

1. Samuel Eliot Morrison, et al, Growth of the American Republic, vol. II (N.Y.: Oxford Univesity Press, 1980), p. 180-181. Hereafter cited as Morrison, vol. II.

2. Gresham to Blount, March 11, 1893, Blount Report, p. 1185.

3. Russ, vol. I, p. 191.

4. Blount to Gresham, April 8, 1893, Blount Report, p. 476.

5. Stevens to Gresham, April 4, 1893, Blount Report, p. 419.

6. Russ, vol. I, p. 272.

7. Blount to Gresham, May 6, 1893, Blount Report, p. 526.

8. Blount to Gresham, April 6, 1893, Blount Report, p. 472-3.

9. Blount to Gresham, May 6, 1893, Blount Report, p. 526.

10. Blount to Gresham, July 17, 1893, Blount Report, p. 587.
11. Ibid., p. 595.
12. Blount to Gresham, April 8, 1893, Blount Report, p. 476.
13. Blount Report, p. 583.
14. Blount to Gresham, July 17, 1893, Blount Report, p. 581.
15. Ibid., p. 594
16. Ibid., p 599.
17. Ibid., p. 594.
18. Ibid., p. 595.
19. Blount to Gresham, July 17, 1893, Blount Report, p. 572-3.
20. Damon interview, April 29, 1893, Blount Report, p. 510.
21. Blount to Gresham, July 17, 1893, Blount Report, p. 574.
22. Blount to Gresham, May 24, 1893, Blount Report, p. 533.
23. Blount to Gresham, July 17, 1893, Blount Report, p. 585.
24. Trousseau statement, May 16, 1893, p. 992.
25. Blount to Gresham, July 17, 1893, Blount Report, p. 585.
26. Blount to Gresham, May 6, 1893, Blount Report, p. 527.
27. Blount to Gresham, July 17, 1893, Blount Report, p. 586.
28. Lili'uokalani statement, Blount Report, p. 869.
29. Ibid., p. 865.
30. Ibid., p. 869.
31. Thurston to Dole, June 13, 1893, Thurston, p. 297-300.
32. Smith to Thurston, September 21, 1894, William Adam Russ, Jr., The Hawaiian Republic 1894-1898, (Selinsgrove, Pennsylvania: Susquehanna University Press, 1959), p. 51. Hereafter cited as Russ, vol. II.
33. Blount Report, p. 911.
34. Thurston to Dole, November 19, 1893, Thurston, p. 339-340.
35. Gresham to Schurz, September 14, Osborne, p. 50.
36. Gresham to Butler, November 23, 1893, Osborne, p. 57.
37. Russ, vol. I, p. 228.
38. Gresham to Willis, October 18, 1893, Blount Report, p. 1190.
39. Ibid., p. 1190-1191.
40. Willis to Gresham, November 16, 1893, Blount Report, p. 1242.
41. Willis to Gresham, December 3, 1893, Blount Report, p. 1191-1192.
42. Ibid.
43. Russ, vol. I, p. 253.
44. Gresham to Willis, November 24, 1893, Blount Report, p. 1191.
45. Ibid., vol. I, p. 254.
46. Willis to Gresham, December 9, 1893, Russ, vol. I, p. 255-6.
47. Ibid. p. 254.
48. Lili'uokalani, p. 246-248.
49. Congressional Research Service, The Library of Congress, "Present Civilian Federal Death Penalty Statutes, p. 3, May 30, 1989.
50. Gresham to Cleveland, October 18, 1893, Blount Report, p. 462.
51. Ibid., p. 463.

52. Cleveland message, December 18, 1893, Blount Report, p. 445-458.

53. Russ, vol. I, p. 265.

54. Dole to Willis, December 18, 1893, Blount Report, p. 1280.

55. Gresham to Willis, January 12, 1894, Blount Report, p. 1283.

56. *Hawaiian Star,* January 18, 1894, Willis to Gresham, January 19, 1894, Blount Report, p. 1207.

57. Osborne, p 73.

58. 53 Congress 2nd Session, Congressional Record, p. 2001-7.

59. Stevens statement, Morgan Report, vol. II, p. 550.

60. Ibid., p. 521 and 329.

61. Morgan Report, vol. I, p. 2.

62. Ibid., p. 21.

63. Ibid., p. 20.

64. Ibid., p. 7.

65. Ibid., p. 20.

66. Ibid., p. 6.

67. Osborne, p. 81.

68. Alan Nevins, Grover Cleveland A Study in Courage, (New York: Dodd, Mead and Co., 1934), p. 561.

69. Thurston to Dole, November 19, 1893, Thurston, p. 339.

70. Willis to Gresham, November 18, 1893, Blount Report, p. 435-436.

71. Russ, vol. I, p. 135.

72. Skerrett, June 28, 1893, Morgan Report, vol. II, p. 2216.

73. Blount Report, p. 510, and Russ, vol. II, p. 26.

74. Allen, p. 341.

75. Russ, vol. II, p. 63.

Annexation

1. H. Wayne Morgan, William McKinley and His America. (Syracuse: Syracuse University Press, 1963), p. 295. Hereafter cited as H. Morgan.

2. Conroy, p. 136.

3. Osborne, p. 28.

4. Ibid., p. 34.

5. Blount Report, p. 542.

6. Morrison, vol. II, p. 259.

7. Sylvester Stevens, p. 144.

8. Thompson, p. 84.

9. Hatch to Cooper, December 6 and 10, 1897, Russ, vol. II, p. 216.

10. Dole to Cooper, January 18, 1898, Russ, vol. II, p. 231.

11. H. Morgan, p. 301.

12. NHSC, vol. I, p. 302.

13. Ibid.

14. Ibid., p. 303.

15. Ibid.

16. Russ, vol. II, p. 305.
17. Ibid.
18. Ibid.
19. NHSC, vol. I, p. 302.
20. Ibid., p. 302-303.
21. Ibid., p. 304.
22. Russ, vol. II, p. 352-353.
23. Charles Tansill, The Foreign Policy of Thomas F. Bayard, (New York: Fordam University Press, 1940), p. 409.

Was Annexaton Legal?

1. NHSC, vol. I, p. 305.
2. Ibid., p. 306.
3. Ibid., p. 306.
4. H. Morgan, p. 296.
5. Ibid., p. 295.
6. Merze Tate, The United States and the Hawaiian Kingdom, (Westport, Connecticut: Greenwood Press, 1965), p. 273.
7. NHSC, vol. I, p. 308.
8. 105 Congressional Record, pp. 14564-16566 (1959).
9. Lawrence Fuchs, Hawaii Pono: A Social History (New York: Harcourt, Brace and World, Inc., 1961), p. 179.

Index

About the Author

Rich Budnick received a B.A. Degree in History and Political Science from UCLA and a M.A. Degree in Government from California State University, Sacramento.

This is his third book as an author and a self-publisher.

His previous two books were: **Hawaiian Street Names:** The Complete Guide to Oʻahu Street Names (with Duke Kalani Wise) and **Maui Street Names:** The Hawaiian Dictionary and History of Maui Street Names (with Hōkūlani Holt-Padilla). He has sold more than 12,000 copies of these books.

Budnick works as a Public Information Officer for Hawaiʻi state government. Previously he worked as the Maui County Information Officer, and as a Legislative Assistant for the California State Legislature.